Measuring Social Attitudes

A Handbook for Researchers and Practitioners

Fred Leong
Department of Psychology
Southern Illinois University
Carbondale, Illinois 62901

Measuring Social Attitudes

A Handbook for Researchers and Practitioners

DANIEL J. MUELLER
Indiana University

Teachers College, Columbia University
New York and London

Published by Teachers College Press, 1234 Amsterdam Avenue, New York, N.Y. 10027

Library of Congress Cataloging in Publication Data

Mueller, Daniel J., 1940–
  Measuring social attitudes.

  Bibliography: P.
  Includes index.
  1. Attitude (Psychology)—Testing.   I. Title.
II. Title: Social attitudes.
BF323.C5M84   1986   303.3'8'072   85-26175
ISBN 0-8077-2804-7
ISBN 0-8077-2795-4 (pbk.)

Manufactured in the United States of America

91 90 89   2 3 4 5 6

Contents

Preface

This book is about measuring social attitudes. It is designed as a comprehensive and detailed handbook for the construction, selection, and evaluation of a wide variety of attitude-measurement instruments and procedures. In writing this book I have tried to address myself to applied researchers and practitioners without a great deal of statistical or psychometric sophistication. The entire book is written in an easy-to-read, conversational style yet with careful attention to technical accuracy. Nearly every chapter contains figures and tables illustrating the techniques and procedures described.

Primary emphasis is on the well-known scaling techniques of Thurstone, Likert, Guttman, and Osgood (Chapters 2–6). Almost anybody, starting from scratch, can construct attitude scales of high quality by following the procedures outlined in these chapters.

In Chapter 7 standard reliability and validity procedures are reviewed, and their application to attitude measures is discussed. About two-thirds of this chapter is devoted to predictive and construct validity. Thorough and extensive discussion of the predictability of human behavior from attitude scores is followed by a review of multiple procedures for establishing that the attitude construct is indeed being measured.

Chapter 8 is a potpourri of measurement techniques that are alternative to the standard scaling techniques covered in earlier chapters. These alternate techniques vary greatly, from additional multi-item scaling procedures to measurement with a single item, from other self-report techniques to observational and interviewing methods, from highly disguised to blatantly direct techniques, and from highly structured to highly unstructured procedures. Even physiological measures are presented as a possible index of attitude.

A highly palatable dose of theory is introduced in Chapter 1 in order to lay a conceptual foundation for measurement of the attitudinal construct. A definition for *attitude* is established, and its relationship to kindred psychological constructs is discussed. In Chapter 9, "Conclusions," the nature of attitude is again reviewed. This time a more formal model of the belief-attitude-value interrelationship (Fishbein's model) is presented, and the dimensionality of the attitude construct is pondered.

This book can serve as a primary text in attitude-measurement courses. It will also be useful as a supplementary text for courses in psychological and educational measurement, psychometric theory, research methodology, social psychology, and personality. It is a handy reference work for attitude researchers in all fields of social science as well as for applied researchers in professional fields.

Measuring Social Attitudes

A Handbook for Researchers and Practitioners

1

The Nature of Attitude

What is your attitude concerning the availability of handguns to the civilian public?

"Handguns are involved in a high proportion of killings in this country. I believe the public should not be allowed to buy handguns."

"I own a Colt .38 and I intend to keep it."

"I hate guns."

"In my opinion guns don't kill people; people kill people."

"I feel that it is my inalienable right to bear arms, and that includes handguns."

"All handguns should be dumped into the deepest part of the ocean."

"It doesn't matter to me one way or the other."

"My attitude is mostly negative. I do not think that handguns should be available to the public."

"I favor the registration of handguns."

"I've owned a pistol for 20 years and have never harmed a hair on anyone's head."

When asked about their "attitude," people respond with *opinions, beliefs, feelings, prescriptions* (behavioral preferences or behavioral intentions), statements of *fact*, and statements about their own *behavior*. They make highly *cognitive* responses, and they make highly *affective* responses. Apparently all these psychological concepts are part of the attitude domain and are associated with attitude in some way.

ATTITUDE AS A PSYCHOLOGICAL CONSTRUCT

Attitude is a psychological construct. Like all psychological constructs, attitude is hypothetical. Constructs are ways of conceptualizing intangible elements of the domain studied by a particular science. Social scientists study the beliefs and behaviors of people in an effort to draw inferences about mental states and mental processes. Attitudes cannot be observed or measured directly. Their existence must be inferred from their consequences.

In order to be useful to scientists in the study of the universe (including the social and psychological domains of the universe), a construct must meet certain criteria. First, it must have a precise and unambiguous definition. And consonant with this definition, the relationship of the construct to other elements of the domain under consideration must be established. Specifically, its distinctiveness from, as well as its similarity to, related constructs must be articulated. In combination, the construct definition and the specification of its relationship to other elements of the universe (including other constructs) are sometimes referred to as the "theory of the construct" or its "nomological net." In the case of the construct *attitude,* it is important to establish its distinctiveness from, and/or similarity to, such other psychological constructs as *belief, opinion, interest, set, value,* and *behavior.* These aspects of the nomological net of the attitude construct will be discussed at various points in the following chapters.

Psychological constructs must also be observable or measurable by some means in order to be useful to social scientists. If they are not measurable, they cannot be used in scientific research. Hypotheses concerning their causes and effects cannot be tested, and their relationships to other constructs cannot be proven or disproven.

Social scientists in general, and psychologists in particular, have had a difficult time developing constructs that meet these criteria. The human mind is very complex, and the affective domain within the human psyche seems particularly resistant to being categorized, organized, labeled, and understood. To make matters worse, many of the construct names used by psychologists are already in use by lay people. In fact, there are literally thousands of adjectives used in everyday language to describe mental traits and conditions. Many of these are not technically defined and are used with greater or lesser degrees of consistency.

Attitude exemplifies this dilemma. The word *attitude* is used with many different definitions, or with no clear definition at all, in everyday language. Even social scientists are not in complete agreement regarding a definition. In any particular theoretical or research application, including this book, a precise definition must be established for the enterprise to proceed fruitfully.

ATTITUDE DEFINED

While there is not total consensus among social scientists regarding the definition of *attitude,* there is substantial agreement that *affect for or against* is a critical component of the attitude concept. Looking back through all of the quotations in response to the question "What is your attitude concerning the availability of handguns to the civilian public?" you will see that every response either states directly or implies a positive or a negative affect toward the availability of handguns to the civilian public. (The only exception is the response "It doesn't matter to me one way or the other." But this implies a neutral attitude—a position that also can be located on the positive-negative affective continuum.)

Louis Thurstone is the social psychologist credited with first formalizing and popularizing an attitude-measurement methodology. Thurstone scales remain, to this day, a standard instrument in the arsenal of attitude-measurement technology. In 1928 Thurstone defined *attitude* as "the sum total of a man's inclinations and feelings, prejudice and bias, preconceived notions, ideas, fears, threats, and convictions about any specified topic" (p. 531). But in 1931 he said simply, "Attitude is the affect for or against a psychological object" (p. 261). In 1946 he indicated that he wished he had retained the more limited definition of *attitude* contained in a draft of his 1928 paper: "the intensity of positive or negative affect for or against a psychological object"(p. 39).

This book adopts Thurstone's definition. It can be restated in any of the following ways. *Attitude* is (1) affect for or against, (2) evaluation of, (3) like or dislike of, or (4) positiveness or negativeness toward a psychological object.

To be sure, there are many other definitions of *attitude*—almost as many, in fact, as there are theorists in the attitude arena. I adhere to the Thurstone definition for three reasons. First, while some definitions of *attitude* are much more elaborate, virtually all contain the essence of Thurstone's definition. Beyond this, disagreement becomes widespread.

In the second place, many definitions of *attitude* include a reference to behavior or to a tendency or "set" to respond or to behave in a certain manner. An excerpt from a 1931 definition by Emory Bogardus states that "an attitude is a tendency to act toward or against some environmental factor" (p. 45). And in a much quoted 1935 definition, Gordon Allport indicates that "an attitude is a mental or neural state of readiness" (p. 810). Similarly, Donald Campbell defines *attitude*, in part, as "consistency in response to social objects" (Campbell, 1950, p. 31). The uncertainty of attitude theorists regarding whether to incorporate a reference to behavior or response set in the definition of *attitude* is clearly illustrated in a definition by Ralph Linton, a renowned cultural anthropologist. According to Linton, "an attitude may be defined as the *covert response* [emphasis mine] evoked by a value" (Linton, 1945, pp. 111–12). In Chapters 2 and 7, I will discuss in more depth the relation of behavior to attitude. Suffice it to say for now that behavior and attitude are separate psychological phenomena. While they may, under certain conditions, be highly related, they are not always highly related and should not be expected to be. Thus it is inappropriate to include one in the definition of the other. We will see in the next chapter that statements about *tendency* to behave or *set* to respond can be used as *indices* of attitude, but that does not legitimate inclusion of this tendency in the *attitude* definition. I prefer to leave *tendency to respond* out of the *attitude* definition because of its obvious behavior-prediction implications. Whether attitude does or does not predict behavior (in specific social situations) is an important scientific question. This question can best be addressed by testing directly the relationship of attitude to actual behavior. The notion of response *tendency* seems to add no conceptual richness to the *attitude* definition.

My third reason for sticking with a very simple definition of *attitude* is that this is what is measured in the popularly used attitude scales. Many hundreds of research studies have been conducted using the measurement techniques developed by Thurstone, Likert, Borgardus, Guttman, and Osgood. These instruments, either by design or by default, have used the very simple, one-dimensional definition proffered by Thurstone. Attitude theories, meanwhile, have suggested that attitude is a much more complex and multidimensional construct.

The interdependence of theory and data is a commonly accepted phenomenon in the philosophy of science. Theory determines the nature of the data to be collected, defines constructs, and influences the selection and development of data-collection instruments. Data, in turn, bring about changes in theoretical propositions and hypotheses and the reconceptualization of theoretical constructs. In the realm of attitude, however, measurement and theory have, unfortunately, developed somewhat independently.

THE RELATION OF ATTITUDES TO VALUES

Value is an important construct in virtually every branch of social science, as well as in the fields of economics, philosophy, theology, education, and counseling. It is a primary construct for theory and research in the disciplines of sociology and anthropology. One might expect that with such prominence and popularity among scientists and practitioners the value construct would enjoy a clear and well-established definition. Unfortunately, such is not the case. In fact, there is less consensus regarding the definition of *value* than of *attitude*. In part, this is because *value* is used in different ways and for different theoretical purposes, from discipline to discipline. The other reason that the construct *value* suffers from lack of definitional consensus is that it is a more abstract construct than *attitude* and thus is harder to conceptualize clearly.

As with *attitude*, though, there are common threads running through the prominent *value* definitions. Two of the most popular definitions will serve well here to identify the critical elements of the value construct. Clyde Klukhohn, a well-known anthropologist, has defined *value* as "a conception, explicit or implicit, distinctive of an individual or characteristic of a group, of the desirable, which influences the selection of available modes, means, and ends of action" (Klukhohn, 1965, p. 395). In a more recent but somewhat similar definition, Milton Rokeach, a social psychologist, states that *value* is an "enduring belief that a specific mode of conduct or end state of existence is personally or socially preferable to an opposite or converse mode of conduct or end state of existence" (Rokeach, 1973, p. 5).

Like attitudes, values involve evaluating. But it is generally agreed among social theorists that values are more abstract, higher-order constructs than are attitudes. They are thus more permanent and resistent to change, and they have a direct or indirect causal influence on both attitudes and behaviors. Both Klukhohn and Rokeach have indicated that values may express either personal or social preferences and that values may serve either as ends (goals) or as means to ends—both common distinctions among value theorists.

There is general agreement that values cause attitudes. More specifically, an attitude toward an object is a function of the extent to which that object is perceived to facilitate the attainment of important values. For example, if an athlete values privacy and independence but disvalues structure, she may have a more positive attitude toward individual sports such as tennis and track than toward group sports such as basketball and soccer. Likewise, one's attitudes toward persons, groups, and *all* cognitive objects (houses, spouses, books, restaurants, automobiles, fishing poles, suspenders, countries, cat foods, and so forth) will be determined largely by the extent to which each of these objects is associated with the fulfillment of his values.

Thus values are determinants of attitudes. Let us be clear, though, that there is not a one-to-one relationship between particular attitudes and particular values. Rather, a single attitude is "caused" by many values—by one's whole value system, in fact. One more example will serve to crystallize this understanding. If I am shopping for a new car, my value system tells me the relative importance of economy, power, comfort, durability, roominess, safety, style, and so forth. My attitude toward a particular car (in fact, toward *every* particular car) is determined by my hierarchical ordering of these values and by my beliefs regarding the extent to which each car is associated with the fulfillment of each value.

THE RELATION OF ATTITUDES TO BELIEFS

Some attitude theorists have stressed the importance of *beliefs* in their conceptualizations of attitude. Newcomb, for example, calls attitudes "stored cognitions that have some positive or negative associations" (Newcomb, Turner, & Converse, 1965, p.40). Our beliefs about things affect the way we feel about them. If we believe an individual has many good qualities, we tend to like him. Our beliefs, in turn, are influenced by our attitudes. We are more willing to believe, or even assume, positive information about persons whom we like than about persons we don't like. This reciprocal relationship between cognition and affect is useful to scientists in the measurement of attitude. Rather than just asking respondents how they *feel* about a particular attitudinal object, attitude measurers can ask what they *believe* about the object. Belief statements almost always contain an affective component. A respondent with lots of positive beliefs and only a few negative beliefs about a psychological object is judged to have a positive attitude. One with many negative beliefs and few positive ones has a negative attitude. The attitude-measurement techniques developed by Thurstone, Likert, and Guttman (described in subsequent chapters) are really just systematic methods of abstracting the affective component of belief statements to effect an attitude score.

In recent decades several attitude theorists have developed mathematical equations to explain the relative contribution of each belief about an attitudinal object to attitude toward that object. The two major elements in these equations are (1) the magnitude of the particular value associated with the attitudinal object in each belief statement and (2) the extent to which the statement is believed (i.e., the extent to which the attitudinal object is believed to be associated with that value). Works by Rosenberg (1956) and Fishbein (1967a) exemplify these attitude models. They will be examined in greater detail after we have reviewed a variety of attitude-measurement methods and procedures (Chapter 9).

THE IMPORTANCE OF ATTITUDE IN HUMAN AFFAIRS

In studying the processes of social perception, human learning, concept formation, personality development, and attitude formation, psychologists have discovered that human beings *evaluate* just about everything they come into contact with: other people, animals, inanimate objects, institutions, groups, and so forth. If you don't believe it, look around you. Let your mind settle on any object, from a pencil to a person, and ask yourself, "How do I feel about this object?" Almost surely your answer will indicate the extent to which you like or dislike, value or disvalue, the object. Of course, your feelings about pencils may not be as strong as your feelings about persons. Nonetheless, you may very well be able to decide that you like one pencil better than another pencil. That's attitude—evaluation; extent of liking or disliking; positive or negative feeling; and valuing or disvaluing of particular, specified objects.

In the 1950s Charles Osgood and his associates at the University of Illinois carried out cross-cultural research into the nature of meaning. It was Osgood's belief that there is substantial connotative overlap or redundancy in the myriad of adjectives that we use to describe the world around us. In a series of experiments Osgood had hundreds of subjects from several countries respond to scores of adjective descriptions of a large number of psychological objects. Through application of a complex statistical procedure, called factor analysis, Osgood determined that the major portion of the essence of meaning is accounted for by three dimensions: evaluation, potency, and activity. Of the three, evaluation is by far the largest component of meaning. Most social psychologists, including Osgood, equate the evaluation dimension with attitude. The data-collection instrument used by Osgood in this research is called the *semantic differential* (Osgood, Suci, & Tannenbaum, 1957). Its use specifically as an attitude-measurement instrument is described in Chapter 6.

It is no wonder that researchers and practitioners in education and social science have spent enormous amounts of time and energy in the study of attitude formation and change and of the effects of attitudes on behavior. Attitudes constitute an immensely important component in the human psyche. They strongly influence all of our decisons: the friends we pick, the jobs we take, the movies we see, the foods we eat, the spouses we marry, the clothes we buy, and the houses we live in. We choose the things we choose, to a large extent, because we *like* them.

2
Likert Attitude Scaling

Measuring someone's attitude is an attempt to locate his position on an affective continuum ranging from "very positive" to "very negative" toward an attitudinal object. In the Likert scaling technique this quantification is accomplished by tallying respondents' affirmation of positive and negative belief statements about the attitudinal object.

DELIMITING THE ATTITUDINAL OBJECT

In the discussion of the nature and definition of *attitude* in Chapter 1, frequent reference was made to the "psychological object" or "attitudinal object." *Attitude*, it was indicated, is the extent of liking or disliking something. That "something" is the attitudinal object. The first consideration in *any* attempt at attitude measurement is to identify this object. "Attitude toward what?" is the question that must be answered before proceeding farther. The more precisely the attitudinal object is delimited, the more successful will be the measurement effort. In order for attitude-scale scores to be meaningful, it is essential for the researcher who uses the scale scores to have precisely the same object in mind as do the respondents to the scale. Similarly, the scale-construction effort will not be successful if the attitudinal object is so nebulous or ill defined that different respondents have slightly different objects in mind.

In general, simple objects are more easily delimited than are complex objects, tangible objects are more easily delimited than are abstract objects, and individual, particular objects are more easily delimited than are classes of objects. Proper nouns are among the easiest objects to work with: Martin Luther King, Honda Accord, Statue of Liberty. But attitude measurement would be of limited practical value if we were restricted to measuring attitude toward simple, tangible objects.

In measuring attitudes toward complex and/or abstract objects, it is vitally important to define the object thoroughly and completely. If you want to measure attitude toward *education*, for instance, you must be clear in your own mind, and in communication with others (scale respondents, consumers of your research findings, and so forth) which of the following components are included in your definition of *education:*

1. The general level of societal literacy (e.g., "A highly educated society makes a strong country.")
2. Education as a profession (e.g., "Education is a fulfilling profession.")
3. The public school system (e.g., "Formal education in this country is the best in the world.")
4. One's own educational level (e.g., "More education will make me a better person.")

If you included all these items in a single scale and summed item scores for each respondent, the total scores would have little or no clear meaning. The solution is either to construct multiple scales, one for each attitudinal object, or to define *education* narrowly and specifically enough so that some of these multiple dimensions are precluded. Rather than bothering scale respondents with a definition, such delimitation of the attitudinal object is generally accomplished through careful selection of scale items.

GENERATING AN ITEM POOL

Once the attitudinal object has been determined, a pool of items stating beliefs or opinions about that object is constructed or collected. It is important, in generating this item pool, to tap a broad diversity of opinions about the attitudinal object. Since completed Likert scales typically contain only about 20 of the dozens or even hundreds and thousands of possible beliefs about a particular object, they will be most valid if they constitute a fairly comprehensive and representative sampling of this almost infinite theoretical domain. One way to achieve this comprehensiveness in generating potential scale items is to ask a diverse group of people (those with substantial knowledge about, and with both positive and negative attitudes toward, the attitudinal object) to write down several of their own beliefs and feelings about the attitudinal object. With a little editing, belief statements generated in this manner can become the item pool that serves as the basis for your attitude scale. Interviews and other conversations about the attitudinal object are similarly productive in generating useful pool items, as are editorial-type writings about the object.

While in a broad sense all attitudinal items can be called *belief* or *opinion* statements, attitude measurers sometimes distinguish among belief or *cognitive* items, feeling or *affective* items, and behavioral-tendency or *conative* items. Cognitive items express beliefs about the attitudinal object.

Affective items constitute a very direct expression of feeling toward the attitudinal object. Conative items express behavioral intention or behavioral preference with regard to the object. There are actually two kinds of behavioral-tendency items: *would* items and *should* items. Would items express a personal behavioral intention toward the attitudinal object. Should items express a behavioral preference for social action. Following are examples of these various item types, with diesel cars the attitudinal object:

> Belief: Diesel cars are economical to run.
> Feeling: I like diesel cars.
> Would: I would buy a diesel car if I had my choice.
> Should: The government should give a tax credit to people who buy diesel cars.

Since beliefs about, feelings toward, and behavioral tendencies with regard to objects tend to be highly related (people who like *X* tend to have positive beliefs about *X* and to express tendencies or desires to behave positively toward *X*), any or all of these types of items can be used in attitude scales, without distinction.

It is important, however, to distinguish between *behavioral-tendency* items and *actual-behavior* items. Actual-behavior items can be somewhat of a problem in attitude scales. Someone living in Alaska might think diesel cars are "the greatest" but might have to respond "no" or "disagree" to the statement "I own a diesel car," because diesel cars are not generally available in Alaska. If you think about it, you'll realize that actual behaviors are influenced by many things besides attitudes and therefore are not always accurate indices of attitude. As a general rule, items inquiring about respondents' actual behaviors are best left out of attitude scales. A more thorough discussion of the relation of attitude to behavior is found in Chapter 7.

Each Likert item should be clearly positive or negative with regard to the attitudinal object. Neutral items won't work in Likert scales. Positive items are items that state favorable beliefs about or feelings toward the attitudinal object. Following are examples of positive, neutral, and negative items:

> Positive: I would prefer having a diesel-powered car. Diesel cars use less fuel.
> Neutral: Diesel cars are a kind of automobile. Diesel cars are produced in the U.S.
> Negative: Diesel cars don't start easily in cold weather. Diesel cars cost more than they are worth.

Some items may connote a positive attitude for some respondents but a negative attitude for others. For example, the item "I like diesel cars about as well as I like tutti-frutti ice cream" is as positive or as negative as tutti-frutti ice cream is to each respondent. Care should be taken to select only items for which there is a very high degree of consensus regarding the direction (positive or negative) of the affective component. An objective method for making this determination is described later in this chapter, in the section entitled "Item Analysis."

Another type of item that won't benefit your scale is an item to which all respondents make the same response. When your scale is complete, it will be used to discriminate among respondents, that is, to distinguish people with very positive attitudes from those with moderately positive attitudes, and these, in turn, from those with negative attitudes, and so forth. Every item must contribute a little to this discrimination. In order to discriminate, items must "spread people out" in terms of score points. If all respondents make the same response to an item, the item isn't spreading them out. In the extreme case, if all respondents make the same response to every item in the scale, they will all obtain the same total score. There will be no discrimination whatsoever, and the scale will be useless.

Some factual items don't spread respondents out. If a fact is so well established that all respondents "agree," it won't make a good attitudinal item. For example, probably all or nearly all respondents would "strongly agree" that "diesel cars burn diesel fuel." Some factual items, however, can discriminate just fine. It is objectively established that "diesel cars get better mileage per gallon than do gasoline cars," but not all respondents know and/or believe this fact. Those who know this positive "fact" will agree and thus have legitimate points added to their attitude score. Those who have misinformation will disagree and thus not gain attitudinal points. Those who don't know may answer "uncertain" or may guess based upon their overall attitude toward diesel cars. A factual item such as this can spread respondents out and thus *will* contribute to the discrimination of the scale.

Strongly or extremely worded items can also suffer from the problem of not spreading respondents out. The item "I would never purchase a diesel car" won't spread people out as well as this less extremely worded rewrite: "I am unlikely to purchase a diesel car." In general, the use of absolutes such as *always* and *never* should be avoided in writing Likert scale items. Of course, you'll know better how well your items are spreading people out *after* you administer them, but even before administration you can be on the lookout for items that state well-established facts and items that are very strongly worded.

It should be clear, by now, that good item writing is in large part simply a matter of good writing. The wording of each item must convey the same meaning to the respondent that it conveys to the item writer. Furthermore, it must convey the same meaning to all respondents. Items should be worded as briefly, as clearly, and as concisely as possible.

A particular problem for respondents in taking attitude scales is compound items (Likert called these "double-barreled" items). Compound items really contain two beliefs or opinions in one sentence, for example, "Diesel cars are noisy and smelly." Respondents may agree with one part of the statement (one belief) and disagree with the other part. Two potentially good items on a scale measuring attitude toward diesel cars could be constructed from this double-barreled statement.

About half positive and half negative items is the proportion usually recommended in order to preclude the possible effect of "acquiescence response set." (A thorough discussion of response sets appears in Chapter 7.)

A final consideration in constructing the item pool is how many items to include. The answer depends partly on how well your items are written, partly on how specific your attitudinal object is, and partly on how reliable you need your final scale to be. If you are a novice at writing and editing items for attitude scales, you may need to start out with a pool of more than 50 items. If you have been systematically editing items and eliminating poorly worded and redundant items during the item-pool construction process, and if you are a good writer, you may need only 25 or 30 items in your initial pool. Attitudes toward specific and "tightly" conceptualized objects can be measured accurately with fewer items than attitudes toward loosely defined and amorphous objects. The question of reliability will be discussed at length in Chapter 7. Suffice it to say here that, all else being equal, the magnitude of the reliability coefficient is directly related to scale length.

RESPONSE FORMAT AND SCORING

Likert items use response categories ranging from "strongly agree" through "strongly disagree." Five categories are fairly standard ("strongly agree," "agree," "uncertain" or "undecided," "disagree," and "strongly disagree"). Some scale constructors use seven categories, and some prefer four or six response categories (with no middle category). All of these options seem to work satisfactorily. It should be noted in this regard that reducing the number of response categories reduces the spreading out of scores (reduces variance) and thus tends to reduce reliability. Increasing the number of response categories adds variance. As the number of response categories is increased, a point is reached at which respondents can no longer reliably distinguish psychologically between adjacent categories (e.g., "Do you agree very strongly, or very, very strongly?"). Increasing the number of categories beyond this point simply adds random (error) variance to the score distribution.

In scoring positively stated Likert items "strongly agree" receives 5 points, "agree" 4 points, and so on. For negatively worded items the scoring is reversed ("strongly agree" equals 1, "agree" equals 2, and so on). Thus, responses indicating a positive attitude toward the attitudinal object (agree responses to positive items; disagree responses to negative items) result in high scale scores. Responses indicating a negative attitude toward the attitude object result in low scale scores. In calculating the total scale score for each respondent, item scores are summed. (Thus the Likert scaling procedure is commonly known as the method of "summated" ratings.)

The highest possible scale score is $5 \times N$ (number of items). This would certainly be interpreted as a strongly positive attitude. The lowest possible score, indicating a strongly negative attitude, is $1 \times N$. A neutral attitude would result in a score of approximately $3 \times N$. More precise score interpretation should be normative (i.e., relative to the scores of other respondents) rather than "absolute." It is not necessarily true, for instance, that scores above $3 \times N$ are "high" scores. With reference to some attitudinal objects (e.g., democracy, motherhood, apple pie) most or all respondents may score higher than $3 \times N$.

ITEM ANALYSIS

In order to refine the item pool into a finished scale, item analysis is necessary. Following administration of the item pool to a group of respondents, three sets of statistics are typically computed for each item: (1) percentage of respondents making each response, (2) item mean and standard deviation, and (3) item discrimination index. In addition, item analysis usually entails computing a reliability coefficient for the total scale. No fixed number of respondents is required for item analysis, but item and scale statistics will be much more stable when computed on 100 respondents than on 10.

Percentage of respondents making each response to each item and item mean and standard deviation tell about item response distribution, spread, and skew. In general, items on which respondents are spread out across response categories are better than items on which respondents are clustered primarily in two or three response categories. (The problem with well-established factual items, you will remember, is that respondents are not spread out.)

Item discrimination index shows the extent to which each item discriminates among respondents in the same manner as the total scale score. If high scorers on an item have high scale scores and low scorers on the item have low scale scores, the item is discriminating among respondents in the same manner as the total score and thus will have a high discrimination index. In a scale measuring a psychological construct, such as attitude, each item must contribute to the measurement of this construct. Items that don't discriminate among respondents in the same manner as the total score aren't measuring the same thing as the other items. Such items are typically rejected from the scale. When the discrimination index is used as a criterion for rejecting items, the result will be a more homogeneous scale— all remaining items will be contributing to the measurement of the same underlying construct.

If a computer or a somewhat sophisticated calculator is available, correlating item scores with scale scores is the most efficient method of computing item discrimination index. Correlating item scores with total test scores has the same meaning as does intercorrelating any two variables. If the scores on the two variables "go together"—if high scorers on one variable (e.g., test item) tend to be high scorers on the other variable (e.g., total scale) and if low scorers on the one variable tend to be low scorers on the other variable—the variables are positively correlated. Just as in other applications of the correlation statistic, item discrimination indices computed by this method can range from 1.00 to −1.00. Table 2.1 shows the performance of eight students on four test items and on the total test. Try to estimate the correlation of each item with total scale scores.

Item 11 has a very *high, positive* correlation with total scale score. This item discriminates among respondents in the same manner that total score discriminates among respondents. Item 16 has a *moderate, positive* correlation with total score. Item 17 correlates about *zero*, and item 27 has a *moderate* to *high, negative* correlation.

A zero or near zero correlation indicates that the item is discriminating among respondents in a manner unlike the discrimination of the total score (and thus of most of the other scale items). Such an item is not measuring the same thing that the other items are measuring and is not contributing to the measurement being accomplished in the other items. It is usually wise to eliminate such items from the scale. A negatively correlating item is actually working against the discrimination being accomplished in the rest of the scale. A moderate or high negative correlation sometimes signals a miskeyed item (i.e., scored in reverse). If the item has not been miskeyed, it should definitely be removed from the scale.

A more crude, albeit acceptable, method for calculating item discrimination indices is to compare, for each item, the responses made by the high-scoring and low-scoring respondents. Two groups of test takers are selected

TABLE 2.1
Correlating Test Items with Total Scale Score

Respondent	Item 11	Item 16	Item 17	Item 27	Total
James M.	5	4	3	3	92
Marcia W.	5	4	4	2	89
Greg Z.	4	5	2	2	88
Philip H.	3	4	3	3	76
Charlotte A.	2	3	3	4	75
Carlos R.	2	2	2	4	61
Cookie C.	1	2	3	5	60
Mel B.	1	2	4	5	56

on the basis of total scale score, a high-scoring group and an equal-sized low-scoring group. For each item the mean is calculated for each group, and then the mean of the low-scoring group ($\bar{X}_L$) is subtracted from the mean of the high-scoring group ($\bar{X}_H$). Table 2.2 illustrates this procedure for nine items from an attitude scale that was administered to 30 respondents (the middle-scoring 10 respondents are not used in these calculations).

Since the highest possible item score is 5 and the lowest possible item score is 1, the possible range for the *mean difference* discrimination index statistic is from 4.00 to −4.00. A 4.00 can occur only if all high-scoring group members make the most extreme positive item response and all low-scoring group members make the most extreme negative response (as for item 8 in Table 2.2). A −4.00 can occur only with the opposite response pattern. Both are highly unlikely conditions. Items with positive mean differences (i.e., items 1, 2, 3, 5, 6, and 8) are discriminating in a manner similar to the total score. Items with mean differences around zero (items 4 and 9) are not discriminating between high- and low-scoring respondents and are thus not contributing to the measurement of attitude. Items with negative discrimination indices (item 7) are working in opposition to the discrimination being accomplished by the rest of the scale.

There are several possible causes for items failing to discriminate in the same manner as the total scale score. They may be ambiguous in wording, they may be keyed incorrectly (reversing the keying will solve this problem), respondents may not agree about their positiveness/negativeness (reversing the keying for *some* respondents would solve this problem, but

TABLE 2.2
Computation of Discrimination Index via High-scoring Minus Low-scoring Method

Item	High 33% of respondents										High group mean ($\bar{X}_H$)	Low 33% of respondents										Low group mean ($\bar{X}_L$)	Discrimination index ($\bar{X}_H - \bar{X}_L$)
	1	2	3	4	5	6	7	8	9	10		1	2	3	4	5	6	7	8	9	10		
1	5	4	5	5	3	3	4	5	5	5	4.4	3	2	2	1	2	2	1	3	3	2	2.1	2.3
2	5	5	3	4	4	4	3	4	3	4	3.9	3	2	2	2	4	2	4	1	2	2	2.5	1.4
3	4	3	4	4	3	4	3	2	4	5	3.6	2	2	4	3	2	2	2	3	2	2	2.4	1.2
4	3	3	4	3	5	2	3	5	2	2	3.2	3	3	3	2	4	4	4	2	3	3	3.1	0.1
5	4	4	5	4	4	5	5	3	4	3	4.1	1	3	2	3	2	2	1	1	3	2	2.1	2.0
6	5	5	5	5	4	5	5	5	4	5	4.8	1	1	1	2	1	1	1	1	1	2	1.2	3.6
7	3	2	3	2	2	4	2	2	3	1	2.4	4	4	3	4	4	3	4	5	4	5	4.0	-1.6
8	5	5	5	5	5	5	5	5	5	5	5.0	1	1	1	1	1	1	1	1	1	1	1.0	4.0
9	3	2	3	3	4	3	3	2	3	3	2.9	3	3	3	4	3	2	3	3	3	3	3.1	-0.2

that of course is not practical), or they may not connote affect about the attitudinal object at all. Whatever the reason, items with zero and negative discrimination indices should generally be removed from the scale. (Miskeyed items can be kept with rekeying.) The number of items you throw out will depend largely on the size of your initial pool. If you started with a pool of 40 items you can—and probably should—throw out about half. Even many items with good item statistics will be unnecessary. If you began with but a few items to spare in your original pool, it may be necessary to rewrite some items in order to retain a long enough scale for adequate reliability. In reducing scale length on the basis of item statistics, care should be taken to maintain both a diversity of opinion content and a balance of positively and negatively worded items.

A COMPLETED LIKERT SCALE

Figure 2.1 is a standard Likert-type scale designed to measure attitude toward marijuana. Nine items are positive, 11 negative. When the scale was administered in several graduate classes in social psychology, alpha internal consistency reliability coefficients ranged from .83 to .88. (This statistic will be explained in detail in Chapter 7.)

SUMMARY OF LIKERT SCALING PROCEDURES

1. Identify the attitudinal object; delimit it quite specifically.
2. Collect a pool of opinion items (30 or more) about the attitudinal object. All items must state or imply something positive or negative about the attitudinal object. Neutral items cannot be used.
3. Administer the item pool to a group of respondents. Each respondent indicates his degree of agreement to each item.
4. Score each item for each respondent. On a five-point continuum, "strongly agree" receives five points for positive items, "agree" four points, and so forth. For negative items this scoring procedure is reversed.
5. Sum each respondent's item scores. The highest possible score (indicating most positive attitude) is five times the number of items. The lowest possible score is one times the number of items.
6. Correlate total scale scores for all respondents with item scores for all respondents (one item at a time).
7. Eliminate negatively correlating and zero-correlating items. Keep enough positively correlating items to maintain desired level of reliability. Maintain a balance of positive and negative items.

FIGURE 2.1
Likert attitude scale measuring attitude toward marijuana.

Opinions About Marijuana

Indicate on the line to the left of each statement how much
you agree or disagree with it. Please mark every item.
Use the following response categories:

> A = strongly agree
> B = agree
> C = uncertain
> D = disagree
> E = strongly disagree

_____ 1. No right-thinking person would use marijuana. (N)

_____ 2. Marijuana use leads to heroin use. (N)

_____ 3. Only hippies and weirdos use marijuana. (N)

_____ 4. Marijuana should be legalized. (P)

_____ 5. Marijuana use causes birth defects. (N)

_____ 6. Since there is no hangover, marijuana is a good
substitute for alcohol. (P)

_____ 7. Marijuana is a narcotic drug. (N)

_____ 8. Most people who criticize marijuana use don't
know anything about the drug. (P)

_____ 9. Habitual marijuana users are neurotic. (N)

_____ 10. As a symbol of the youth culture, epitomizing
disobedience and disregard for authority,
marijuana usage should be put down. (N)

_____ 11. In our highly impersonal society, marijuana helps
one express feelings and relate to others, and
should therefore definitely be used by those who
feel the need. (P)

_____ 12. Marijuana is a good social stimulator and should
be allowed, especially at parties, where mixing is
important. (P)

_____ 13. Marijuana is not a "hard" drug. (P)

_____ 14. If a son or daughter uses marijuana, Mom and Dad
should be willing to try it before they condemn
it. (P)

FIGURE 2.1 (continued)

_____ 15. Since we aren't sure if it can harm us, we should avoid marijuana. (N)

_____ 16. Marijuana use is illegal and therefore wrong. (N)

_____ 17. Marijuana has psychological therapy potential. (P)

_____ 18. Marijuana causes dehumanization. (N)

_____ 19. Criminals have a higher rate of marijuana use than does the general public. (N)

_____ 20. Intelligence test scores of marijuana users are higher on the average than scores of nonusers. (P)

Note: P = positively keyed item; N = negatively keyed item.

3

Likert Scale Construction

A Case Study

This chapter illustrates the construction of a Likert attitude scale using the procedures described in Chapter 2. The scale-construction project described herein was carried out with the assistance of graduate students in educational and psychological measurement classes who helped in the development of scale items and served as a sample group for the collection of item responses for use in item analysis.

INITIAL SCALE CONSTRUCTION AND ANALYSIS

The attitudinal object selected for this project was *corporal punishment* of children. Forty-seven opinion items about corporal punishment were written and collected by class members. Both positive and negative items were developed, but too many negative items resulted: 31 of 47. An effort was made to include a diversity of opinions, including various perceived social, emotional, and educational consequences of corporal punishment. Most were belief items, but several were behavioral-tendency items—of both the *would* and the *should* types. There were no direct-feeling items. Figure 3.1 is a listing of the 47 items in their administrative format. This initial form of the scale (item pool) was administered to 51 subjects—a convenience sample, consisting of class members and their spouses and friends.

An item analysis of the responses of the 51 subjects was performed by computer.[1] The scale had an alpha reliability coefficient of .96. This is very high reliability. Table 3.1 indicates whether each item was keyed as positive

(Continued on page 29)

---

[1] The SPSS RELIABILITY program was used in this analysis. This program and the EDSTAT TESTAT program (which serves a similar function) are described in Appendix B.

FIGURE 3.1
Initial scale (item pool) for construction of attitude
toward corporal punishment scale.

Opinions About Corporal Punishment

Please answer all items. Use the following response
categories:

                    A = strongly agree
                    B = agree
                    C = undecided
                    D = disagree
                    E = strongly disagree

1. A good teacher would never strike a child. (N)

2. Children who are spanked in school develop bad
   attitudes toward school. (N)

3. Children will respect teachers who have the right to
   paddle them for misbehaving.

4. Corporal punishment is necessary for classroom
   control.

5. Corporal punishment is needed when a child does not
   respond to repeated instructions.

6. Corporal punishment is used by people whose mental
   health is not good. (N)

7. Corporally punishing a student is a motivation for
   good behavior for other students.

8. Corporal punishment is child abuse. (N)

9. Corporal punishment should be abolished by all
   school districts. (N)

10. Corporal punishment in schools leads to violent
    tendencies in the adult population. (N)

11. Schools that use corporal punishment have fewer
    discipline problems than schools that do not.

12. Corporal punishment teaches children that actions
    have consequences.

13. Corporal punishment helps create a disciplined
    atmosphere so that all children can learn.

14. Corporal punishment retards development of
    self-discipline in children. (N)

(continued)

FIGURE 3.1 (continued)

---

15. Corporal punishment creates a repressive atmosphere in the schools. (N)

16. All schools should permit teachers to use corporal punishment in their classrooms.

17. Corporal punishment is a disrespect to the child as a human being. (N)

18. Corporal punishment values the child's conformity but not his/her initiative. (N)

19. The child learns to be aggressive from physical punishment. (N)

20. Spare the rod, spoil the child.

21. When teaching children every day, it will sometimes be necessary to spank them.

22. Corporal punishment is totally ineffective in improving student behavior. (N)

23. Corporal punishment brutalizes the person who administers it. (N)

24. I would allow my child to be physically punished by a teacher for severe misconduct.

25. Corporal punishment makes a hero of the student who is punished. (N)

26. Corporal punishment is acceptable as a last resort.

27. I would never physically punish a student. (N)

28. Corporal punishment causes truancy. (N)

29. Corporal punishment used in the classroom makes parents angry. (N)

30. Corporal punishment produces more negative than positive consequences. (N)

31. Corporal punishment drives a student toward violence. (N)

32. The physically punished pupil learns that aggression is one way to get things done.

33. I always get angry when I hear of a teacher punishing students physically. (N)

FIGURE 3.1 (continued)

---

34. Children learn to behave through the use of physical punishment.

35. A child understands wrongdoing more effectively if he/she is talked to rather than physically abused. (N)

36. I wouldn't allow a teacher to use corporal punishment on my child. (N)

37. Corporal punishment uses aggression to punish aggression. (N)

38. By encouraging corporal punishment in the schools, the students will better understand who has control.

39. Teachers can use corporal punishment as a means of protection from troubled, angry students.

40. Corporal punishment can have grave psychological effects on children. (N)

41. Corporal punishment is abused by teachers. (N)

42. Corporal punishment in the schools can be a positive factor when supported by explanations of the motivation for it.

43. Corporal punishment in the schools leads to imitative behavior of those in the peer group once the punished individual has demonstrated ability to survive in good form. (N)

44. Children hate teachers who hit them. (N)

45. Corporal punishment is necessary in the learning process.

46. Teachers who hurt pupils badly through corporal punishment should be condemned. (N)

47. For teachers to use corporal punishment in front of other pupils is undesirable. (N)

Note: Negatively worded items, to be reversed in scoring, are designated by parenthetical "N" following item.

TABLE 3.1
Means, Standard Deviations, and Discrimination Indices ($\underline{r}$) for Corporal Punishment Opinion Items
(Standardization Sample, $\underline{N}$ = 51)

Item	Positive or negative	Mean	Standard deviation	r with 47-item scale	r with 20-item scale
1. A good teacher would never strike a child.	N	2.16	1.25	.66	--
2. Children who are spanked in school develop bad attitudes toward school.	N	2.59	1.20	.78	.77
3. Children will respect teachers who have the right to paddle them for misbehaving.	P	2.59	1.22	.74	.75
4. Corporal punishment is necessary for classroom control.	P	1.96	1.20	.58	.56
5. Corporal punishment is needed when a child does not respond to repeated instructions.	P	2.20	1.20	.33	--
6. Corporal punishment is used by people whose mental health is not good.	N	3.80	.98	.48	--
7. Corporally punishing a student is a motivation for good behavior for other students.	P	2.59	1.22	.47	--
8. Corporal punishment is child abuse.	N	2.78	1.19	.63	--

Item					
9. Corporal punishment should be abolished by all school districts.	N	2.59	1.36	.92	.93
10. Corporal punishment in schools leads to violent tendencies in the adult population.	N	3.08	1.11	.65	--
11. Schools that use corporal punishment have fewer discipline problems than schools that do not.	P	2.63	1.09	.55	--
12. Corporal punishment teaches children that actions have consequences.	P	3.45	1.10	.50	--
13. Corporal punishment helps create a disciplined atmosphere so that all children can learn.	P	2.55	1.24	.79	.79
14. Corporal punishment retards development of self-discipline in children.	N	2.88	1.11	.73	.66
15. Corporal punishment creates a repressive atmosphere in the schools.	N	2.59	1.37	.55	--
16. All schools should permit teachers to use corporal punishment in their classrooms.	P	2.06	1.30	.72	.71
17. Corporal punishment is a disrespect to the child as a human being.	N	2.55	1.40	.87	.87
18. Corporal punishment values the child's conformity but not his/her initiative.	N	2.65	1.13	.55	--
19. The child learns to be aggressive from physical punishment.	N	2.76	1.18	.44	--

(continued)

TABLE 3.1 (continued)

	Positive or negative	Mean	Standard deviation	r with $\frac{r}{47}$-item scale	r with 20-item scale
20. Spare the rod, spoil the child.	P	2.33	1.16	.48	--
21. When teaching children every day it will sometimes be necessary to spank them.	P	2.27	1.37	.73	.76
22. Corporal punishment is totally ineffective in improving student behavior.	N	2.78	1.20	-.69	.69
23. Corporal punishment brutalizes the person who administers it.	N	2.92	1.25	.73	.73
24. I would allow my child to be physically punished by a teacher for severe misconduct.	P	2.69	1.45	.73	.72
25. Corporal punishment makes a hero of the student who is punished.	N	3.53	1.08	.22	--
26. Corporal punishment is acceptable as a last resort.	P	2.94	1.33	.70	.73
27. I would never physically punish a student.	N	2.41	1.37	.77	.79
28. Corporal punishment causes truancy.	N	3.10	1.02	.58	--
29. Corporal punishment used in the classroom					

Item		Mean	SD		
makes parents angry.	N	2.69	1.01	.37	--
30. Corporal punishment produces more negative than positive consequences.	N	2.37	1.15	.90	.87
31. The physically punished pupil learns that aggression is one way to get things done.	N	2.61	1.18	.41	--
32. I always get angry when I hear of a teacher punishing students physically.	N	2.61	1.27	.72	--
33. Corporal punishment drives a student toward violence.	N	3.00	1.18	.61	--
34. Children learn to behave through the use of physical punishment.	P	2.90	1.28	.61	--
35. A child understands wrongdoing more effectively if he/she is talked to rather than physically abused.	N	1.94	1.08	.63	--
36. I wouldn't allow a teacher to use corporal punishment on my child.	N	2.39	1.44	.78	.80
37. Corporal punishment uses aggression to punish aggression.	N	2.49	1.27	.72	.67
38. By encouraging corporal punishment in the schools, the students will better understand who has control.	P	2 65	1.18	.73	.75
39. Teachers can use corporal punishment as a means of protection from angry students.	P	2.39	1.20	.25	--

(continued)

TABLE 3.1 (continued)

	Positive or negative	Mean	Standard deviation	r with 47-item scale	r with 20-item scale
40. Corporal punishment can have grave psychological effects on children.	N	2.37	1.11	.67	--
41. Corporal punishment is abused by the teachers.	N	2.88	1.03	.43	--
42. Corporal punishment in the schools can be a positive factor when supported by explanations of the motivation for it.	N	3.10	1.36	.79	.81
43. Corporal punishment in the schools leads to imitative behavior of those in the peer group once the punished individual has demonstrated ability to survive in good form.	N	2.67	.97	-.03	--
44. Children hate teachers who hit them.	N	2.92	1.07	.53	--
45. Corporal punishment is necessary in the learning process.	P	1.98	1.05	.74	.73
46. Teachers who hurt pupils badly through corporal punishment should be condemned.	N	1.88	1.03	.41	--
47. For teachers to use corporal punishment in front of other pupils is undesirable.	N	1.98	1.14	.27	--

or negative and lists the item statistics: item means, standard deviations, and correlations with the total (47-item) scale score. All but two items correlated positively with the total score. Item 22 correlated − .69! Rereading the item showed it to be a fairly straightforward negative belief item about corporal punishment: "Corporal punishment is totally ineffective in improving student behavior." Why did it correlate negatively, and so strongly negatively? Perhaps it was mistakenly keyed as a positive item. Examination of the item analysis computer program showed that it was indeed miskeyed. It had been scored as a positive item. If the keying were corrected it would, doubtless, correlate positively with the total score. (It should correlate about + .69 with the total scale score, but not exactly, because the score from this item is included in the total scale score.)

Item 43 correlated − .03. It was keyed as a negative item. Examination showed it to be a negative item, but it is so long and complex that it was probably ambiguous to some respondents: "Corporal punishment in the schools leads to imitative behavior of those in the peer group once the punished individual has demonstrated ability to survive in good form." It had a mean close to 3.00 and the smallest standard deviation of all 47 items: .97. This seems to indicate that many respondents made the "undecided" response. (Unfortunately, the item analysis program that we used did not supply data regarding percentage of responses in each response category for each item.)

The items with the most skewed response distributions appear to be items 4 and 35. The mean responses for these items are more extreme (farther from 3.00) than for any other items. Item 4 is a positive item. Its low mean tells us that the tendency among respondents was to disagree. It has a standard deviation that is about average among the 47 items (1.20). The skewness of its distribution, therefore, probably had relatively little negative impact on its correlation with total score. (Remember that skewness relates to spread of scores, and spread of scores affects correlation.)

Item 35 is a negatively worded item. Its scoring was reversed before the item means were calculated. Therefore a mean of 1.94 indicates that respondents tended to agree. The standard deviation of item 35 is a little smaller than that of item 4 (1.08). Probably it would have correlated more highly with total score had it not been so skewed. (Note in Table 3.1 that there is a general tendency for items with small standard deviations to have relatively low correlations with total score.)

The mean score for the 51 respondents was 123.25. If every respondent had responded "undecided" on every item, the mean would have been 141.00 (47 × 3). A mean of 123.25 indicates that this sample group is somewhat negative in its attitude toward corporal punishment.

REFINING THE SCALE

The next step was to reduce the size of the scale as much as possible, for administrative efficiency, while still retaining high reliability. The amount we need to shorten the scale and the magnitude of reliability we need to retain are judgmental decisions. If we could attain reliability at or near 1.00 with a single item, that is surely what we would do, but the reality is that reliability and scale length tend to be directly related (although removing the few worst items should actually increase reliability).

From the attitude-scaling literature we learn that attitude scales with about 20 items have pretty good reliability (often above .80) if well constructed. For purposes of this exercise we decided to reduce our scale length to 20 items—10 positive and 10 negative. The easiest course is simply to select the 10 highest-correlating positive items and the 10 highest-correlating negative items, so that is what we did. The only exception was keeping item 22—the one with the −.69 correlation. We rekeyed it and kept it in the shortened scale. We reasoned that it would show a high positive correlation if rekeyed, and we were curious to see if we were right.

A second item analysis was run (on the same responses of the 51 sample members) with the refined 20-item scale. Reliability turned out to be .97, *very* high for a 20-item scale. The correlations of these 20 items with the total scale score are also found in Table 3.1. These correlations are slightly different from the original correlations because the total scale score is now the total of the 20-item scale rather than the total of the 47-item scale. The fact that the item–total-score correlations are so similar tells us that almost precisely the same thing is being measured by the two forms of the scale. Notice that our bet paid off on item 22. After rekeying, it correlated with the total scale score .69. (It's just coincidence that both correlations are .69.)

CROSS-VALIDATION

Now we need to see if our reliability will hold up in another sample of respondents. Remember that refining a scale based on a single set of item responses takes advantage of a small amount of interitem correlation that has occurred by chance. In a new sample of respondents, reliability is expected to drop somewhat. Verifying the reliability coefficient across other sample groups is called cross-validation.[2]

---

[2]Cross-validation may also involve the verification of validity data, in other groups.

Accordingly, the refined scale was administered by another class of graduate students to themselves and their friends ($N = 37$). The resultant reliability fell two points, to .95—still very good. Item statistics for the 20-item scale in the cross-validation sample are found in Table 3.2 (see pages 32–33). A comparison of the item–total-score correlations in Tables 3.1 and 3.2 shows that most of these correlations decreased slightly in the cross-validation sample. A few items, such as number 37, had a dramatic decrease in correlation. In a few instances item–total-score correlation increased slightly.

One class member, still a little skeptical, said, "Yes, but what about test-retest reliability?" So we readministered the 20-item scale (eight weeks after the first administration), this time to 11 of the prior 37 (the friends were not all handy, some had not put their names on at the first testing, and we were in a hurry). To our surprise and delight, the test-retest coefficient was .95. We were lucky, I think, to have had some pretty diverse attitudes about corporal punishment represented among class members.

We could have reduced the number of items still further. The reliability would also have been reduced, of course. There is no optimal scale length. Nor, for that matter, is there an optimal level of reliability. As a general rule, when the scores of individuals are being compared, reliability must be very high. When group means are being compared, substantially lower reliability is acceptable.

Ideally we would carry out additional cross-validation studies to determine whether high reliability could be maintained in other sample groups. We don't know, for instance, whether our scale measures attitude toward corporal punishment reliably among high school students or among adults outside of a college setting. Most importantly, we would want to be sure that the scale was highly reliable in groups like the one or ones in which it was intended to be used.

The major remaining question is validity. Is our scale really measuring what we think it is measuring—attitude toward corporal punishment? The topic of validity will be taken up in considerable length in Chapter 7.

TABLE 3.2
Means, Standard Deviations, and Discrimination Indices (r) for Items in Refined Scale
(Cross-validation Sample, N = 37)

Item	Mean	Standard deviation	r with total scale
2. Children who are spanked in school develop bad attitudes toward school.	2.65	.92	.63
3. Children will respect teachers who have the right to paddle them for misbehaving.	2.57	1.09	.73
4. Corporal punishment is necessary for classroom control.	2.27	1.22	.75
9. Corporal punishment is child abuse.	2.59	1.24	.57
13. Corporal punishment helps create a disciplined atmosphere so that all children can learn.	2.27	.96	.65
14. Corporal punishment retards development of self-discipline in children.	2.62	1.06	.63
16. All schools should permit teachers to use corporal punishment in their classrooms.	2.35	1.30	.79
17. Corporal punishment is a disrespect to the child as a human being.	2.46	1.32	.79
21. When teaching children every day, it will sometimes be necessary to spank them.	2.73	1.39	.83

22. Corporal punishment is totally ineffective in improving student behavior.	3.08	1.16	.58
23. Corporal punishment brutalizes the person who administers it.	2.59	.96	.60
24. I would allow my child to be physically punished by a teacher for severe misconduct.	2.49	1.43	.85
26. Corporal punishment is acceptable as a last resort.	3.08	1.40	.79
27. I would never physically punish a student.	2.38	1.32	.49
30. Corporal punishment produces more negative than positive consequences.	2.22	1.08	.72
36. I wouldn't allow a teacher to use corporal punishment on my child.	2.38	1.40	.73
37. Corporal punishment uses aggression to punish aggression.	2.30	1.13	.29
38. By encouraging corporal punishment in the schools, the students will better understand who has control.	2.51	1.02	.60
42. Corporal punishment in the schools can be a positive factor when supported by explanations of the motivation for it.	3.05	1.27	.85
45. Corporal punishment is necessary in the learning process.	1.92	.89	.68

4

Thurstone Scale Construction

Louis Thurstone is considered by many social scientists to be the "father" of attitude scaling. Beginning in the late 1920s Thurstone and several colleagues published a series of articles and monographs that presented the logic of attitude measurement and described and illustrated Thurstone's attitude-scaling methodology.[1] These publications led directly to scholarly revolutions, first in the area of attitude measurement and scaling, and subsequently in the area of empirical research and theory regarding the formation, change, and effects of social attitudes. Indeed, in the decades immediately following the publication of attitude-scaling methodologies by Thurstone, and shortly thereafter by Likert, *attitude* grew to be the single most important construct in social-psychological research and theory.

Thurstone actually developed three separate, albeit related, attitude-scaling techniques: (1) the method of *paired comparisons*, (2) the method of *equal-appearing intervals*, and (3) the method of *successive intervals* (or graded dichotomies). All three methods use the judgments of a panel of judges (who may be any responsible persons) regarding the relative favorableness (positiveness) of attitude statements toward the attitudinal object. Favorableness values for each statement are computed from these judgments, and scale items are selected, based in large part upon these values.

The method of *paired comparisons* (Thurstone, 1927) requires that attitude statements be paired in every possible combination. Each judge then decides which statement in each pair is more favorable toward the attitudinal object. Since 20 statements require the judging of 190 pairs of items, and 40 statements result in 780 pairs, the cumbersomeness of this method is readily apparent. The method of *equal-appearing intervals*, by

---

[1] It should be acknowledged that in 1925 F. Allport and D. Hartman outlined an attitude-scaling technique that is clearly the forerunner of the Thurstone method. In fact, in his 1928 article, Thurstone indicated that his attitude-scaling technique was a refinement of the Allport and Hartman procedure.

comparison, requires judges to sort statements, one at a time, into favor-ableness categories ranging from "extremely unfavorable" to "extremely favorable" (Thurstone & Chave, 1929). Judges are to conceptualize the categories as equidistant (thus the name "equal-appearing intervals"). The method of *successive intervals* (Saffir, 1937) is really an extension of the equal-appearing interval procedure. It is an attempt to establish equal intervals statistically, rather than depending on the subjective estimates of the judges. Using the number of times each statement is assigned by the judges to each favorableness category, the scale constructor is able to calculate the width of each successive interval along the psychological continuum. This method spreads statements out more evenly in scale values, especially at the extremes. The amount of statistical computation involved is worth the effort, though, only if an appropriate computer program is readily available.[2] The scale values of items that result from the successive intervals procedure are very highly correlated with those ob-tained by the equal-appearing intervals procedure.

Only the method of equal-appearing intervals will be described in detail in this book. The method of paired comparisons and the method of successive intervals are described in detail by Edwards (1957).

THE METHOD OF EQUAL-APPEARING INTERVALS

As in Likert scale construction, the first consideration in Thurstone scaling is the identification and careful delimitation of the attitudinal object. The importance of careful delimitation of the attitudinal object was stressed in Chapter 2.

The next step is the accumulation of a pool of opinion statements about the attitudinal object. The criteria for writing, selecting, and editing these statements are almost identical to those outlined for Likert scaling. They will not be repeated here. The only significant difference in criteria is that whereas neutral items are *disallowed* in Likert scale construction, in Thurstone scaling some neutral items are *required*. Thurstone scales, ideally, incorporate a sampling of statements covering the entire evaluative spectrum—from statements extremely favorable to the attitudinal object, through statements that are neutral, to statements extremely unfavorable to the attitudinal object.

It is not possible to prescribe exactly the number of statements needed in

---

[2]See the description of the EDSTAT TSCALE computer program in Appendix B for computation of item favorableness values for Thurstone scales constructed by the successive intervals method.

the initial pool. Thurstone used 130 statements in the pool of one of his earliest published scales. Since that time, however, it has been shown that highly reliable scales can be constructed from substantially smaller item pools, as long as the criteria outlined in Chapter 2 for item selection and editing are followed. It is also advisable to make a special effort to include some neutral and some extremely negative statements in the pool, because these types of statements typically appear most sparsely in attitude item pools. In a first attempt at Thurstone scaling I would recommend beginning with a pool of 40 or 50 opinion statements.

The next step is to obtain favorability values for all statements in the pool. This is done by having a group of judges sort the statements into categories (Thurstone used 11 categories) on a continuum ranging from "extremely unfavorable" to "extremely favorable." Only the most and least favorable and the neutral categories are typically labeled. The categories are successively scored with "extremely unfavorable" having a score of 1 and "extremely favorable" an 11. The scale value of an item is simply the average categorization of that item by all judges. (Medians rather than means are recommended, for a reason we shall see shortly.)

Thurstone used 300 judges, but scales have since been successfully constructed with as few as 10 or 15 judges. Much more important than the number of judges is their degree of concentration on the task. I have found that the judges must be reminded over and over again that they are to respond solely on the basis of the favorableness or unfavorableness of the statements, *not* on the basis of their agreement or disagreement with the statements. Some judges seem to have enormous difficulty maintaining this distinction. In answer to this "response set" problem, Thurstone recommended eliminating the scores of judges who weren't paying attention or who couldn't maintain the appropriate set in making judgments. His rule-of-thumb was to reject all judgments of any judge who placed 30 or more statements (out of 130: 23 percent) into a single category. While this criterion for carelessness is somewhat arbitrary, it *is* important to adopt *some* procedure for the screening of nondiscriminating judges. In addition to extreme skewing of responses by judges, frequent disagreement with other judges signals a careless or inept judge—especially on items where there is strong consensus among the other judges. A further safeguard from irresponsible judges is to compute item medians rather than means when calculating scale values. If, for a particular item, the response of a careless judge is substantially distant from the bulk of the distribution of judgments, the median will be much less affected by this extreme score than will the mean.

There has been substantial debate in the scaling literature regarding criteria for selecting judges. Some evidence exists that judges with extreme attitudinal positions (either very positive or very negative) make fine discriminations among items close to their own position but tend not to discriminate much among the other items, placing them all into a few categories at the opposite end of the continuum. The lesson of these research findings seems to be: Try to use either judges with moderate attitudinal positions or judges from the entire attitudinal range.

Thurstone reproduced the pool items on cards and had judges sort them physically into piles. While this procedure has the advantage of allowing judges to easily check the internal consistency of each pile, it is an extremely cumbersome process. Subsequent researchers have tested a variety of alternative procedures. Three that are logistically more efficient and seem to work just as well as Thurstone's original method, from a psychometric point of view, are illustrated in Figure 4.1. None requires the physical sorting of items.

Another modification of Thurstone's method that appears to be perfectly acceptable is to reduce the number of favorableness categories from 11 to 9 (or even to 7 or 5). While such a reduction of categories has been shown to result in substantially reliable scales, very little is gained in efficiency. Even numbers of categories (e.g., 10, 8, or 6) are seldom used, since this precludes a neutral category.

One more item statistic is necessary before the final scale items can be selected from the pool: a measure of item response variability (i.e., average deviation, standard deviation, or interquartile range). Thurstone reasoned that if an item is ambiguous, there will be poor consensus among judges regarding its degree of favorableness. If there is poor consensus, the item will have a large response variability. Hence, in an effort to avoid ambiguous items, those items with large response variability are excluded from the scale. Thurstone used the interquartile range (Q = 75th percentile − 25th percentile) as his measure of item variability, but standard deviation can quite readily be substituted, especially if you have access to a computer program that computes standard deviation but not one that computes Q. Average deviation will also work for this purpose.

The final scale is constructed by selecting 20 to 25 statements whose median values are approximately equidistant. If a 9-category favorableness scale was used by judges and if 22 items are to be selected for the final scale, the items will need to be picked at scale intervals of approximately .36. (There are 8 units between 1.00 and 9.00; 8 ÷ 22 = .36.) In fact, since no items will have median values as low as 1.00 or as high as 9.00, a slightly smaller interval size, perhaps around .33, should be used to select 22 equidistant items. If two items have the same or nearly the same medians,

(Continued on page 40)

FIGURE 4.1
Three methods of administering statements to be judged in the Thurstone scale
construction process that do not require the physical sorting of items.

a. For each statement, circle the number that indicates the degree of favorableness
of the statement toward the attitudinal object.

| Extremely unfavorable | | Neutral | | | Extremely favorable | | | |

1. Divorce should be encouraged for many unhappily married people.

   1 2 3 4 5 6 7 8 9

2. Divorce brings happiness to some people, unhappiness to others.

   1 2 3 4 5 6 7 8 9

3. Divorce weakens the moral fiber of our society.

   1 2 3 4 5 6 7 8 9

b. For each statement, place a check mark on the adjacent line indicating the
degree of favorableness of the statement toward the attitudinal object.*

| Extremely unfavorable | Neutral | Extremely favorable |

|_____|_____|

1. Divorce should be encouraged for many unhappily married people.

2. Divorce brings happiness to some people, unhappiness to others.

3. Divorce weakens the moral fiber of our society.

c. For each statement, circle the letter that indicates the degree of favorableness of the statement toward the attitudinal object.

Extremely unfavorable			Neutral			Extremely favorable			
A	B	C	D	E	F	G	H	I	J	K

1. Divorce should be encouraged for many unhappily married people.

A B C D E F G H I J K

2. Divorce brings happiness to some people, unhappiness to others.

A B C D E F G H I J K

3. Divorce weakens the moral fiber of our society.

* An 11 (or 9, or 7, and so forth) interval stencil or ruler is superimposed over each line to quantify each judge's rating.

generally the one with the smaller interquartile range (or standard deviation or average deviation) should be chosen—especially if the items have substantially different interquartile ranges.

The chosen items are printed on a form, with instructions to respondents to indicate either agreement or disagreement with each item. The items are usually randomized, but research has shown that printing them in the order of their favorableness values does not adversely affect responses. An example of a completed Thurstone scale appears in Figure 4.2. Each respondent's scale score is the median (or mean) of the values of all items to which he assents. If, for example, a respondent agrees with items 3, 6, 7, and 14 in Figure 4.2, his scale score is 7.25—the median (and in this case also the mean) of the scale values of the four items checked by the respondent.

In Figure 4.3 the items from Figure 4.2 are plotted by scale values. This figure illustrates a severe deficiency in the scale: there are almost no neutral or nearly neutral items. While this attitude scale may suffice for research studies of group comparisons, and to differentiate those respondents with a positive attitude toward open classrooms from those with a negative attitude, it will not discriminate well toward the center of the attitudinal continuum. A specific effort to incorporate more neutral and nearly neutral items in the original item pool would have resulted in a better Thurstone scale.

Figure 4.4 is a scale measuring attitude toward the Chinese. This scale was constructed by Thurstone and published in 1931. A rather elaborate set of instructions acquaints respondents with their task. Not only are respondents required to check (✓) statements with which they agree; they are also to mark statements with which they disagree (with an "X") and for which they are undecided (with a "?"). Since only the checked statements are scored, it is not clear why the other responding procedures were used. If you were to plot the scale values of these 26 items, you would find that they describe a quite evenly spaced scale along the entire attitudinal continuum. Since the highest scale value is 11.5 and the lowest is 0.5, it appears that Thurstone's judges used a 13-point continuum, scored from 0 to 12, in sorting the items. In this scale, low scores indicate positive attitude, high scores negative attitude.

ADVANTAGES AND DISADVANTAGES OF THURSTONE SCALES

Constructing two equivalent forms of an attitude scale is relatively easier in Thurstone scaling than in most other scaling methods. The size of the initial item pool must, of course, be increased, but once the item statistics have been computed, items can be matched (or approximately matched) in

(Continued on page 45)

FIGURE 4.2
Thurstone scale measuring attitude toward open classrooms.

Opinions About Open Classrooms

Check (✓) the statements with which you agree.

____ 1. Open classrooms lead to juvenile delinquency. (1.4)

____ 2. I would not want a child of mine to attend a school with open classrooms. (1.6)

____ 3. Children taught in open classrooms are more creative. (7.9)

____ 4. Open classrooms are too undisciplined for maximum learning. (3.6)

____ 5. Open classrooms are a communist plot. (1.1)

____ 6. Open classrooms facilitate affective development of children. (7.6)

____ 7. Open classrooms positively affect teacher attitude. (6.9)

____ 8. Education in open classrooms is no better and no worse than in ordinary classrooms. (5.0)

____ 9. The noise level in open classrooms is too high to facilitate learning. (3.1)

____10. Open classrooms teach children a sense of responsibility. (7.4)

____11. Principals who promote open classrooms should be replaced. (2.0)

____12. I would vote for a school board candidate who supports the open classroom concept. (7.1)

____13. It should be required by law that all schools adopt the open classroom model of instruction. (8.7)

____14. Children learn more when they have more freedom. (6.6)

____15. Open classrooms result in higher anxiety for some pupils. (2.8)

____16. Open classrooms are just another educational fad. (2.6)

____17. I would sign a petition supporting the use of open classrooms in local elementary schools. (8.2)

Note: Item "favorableness" values appear in parentheses following each item.

FIGURE 4.3
Items from Figure 4.2 plotted by approximate scale values.

9.0

8.5   13. It should be required by law that all schools adopt the open classroom model of instruction. (8.7)

8.0   17. I would sign a petition supporting the use of open classrooms in local elementary schools. (8.2)
       3. Children taught in open classrooms are more creative. (7.9)
       6. Open classrooms facilitate effective development in children. (7.6)

7.5   10. Open classrooms teach children a sense of responsibility. (7.4)
       12. I would vote for a candidate who supports the open classroom concept. (7.1)

7.0   7. Open classrooms positively affect teacher attitude. (6.9)
       14. Children learn more when they have more freedom. (6.6)

6.5

6.0

5.5

5.0   8. Education in open classrooms is no better and no worse than in ordinary classrooms. (5.0)

```
4.5 ─
4.0 ─
3.5 ─    4. Open classrooms are too undisciplined for maximum learning. (3.6)

3.0 ─    9. The noise level in open classrooms is too high to facilitate learning. (3.1)

        15. Open classrooms result in higher anxiety for some pupils. (2.8)
2.5 ─   16. Open classrooms are just another educational fad. (2.6)

2.0 ─   11. Principals who promote open classrooms should be replaced. (2.0)

         2. I would not want a child of mine to attend a school with open classrooms. (1.6)
1.5 ─
         1. Open classrooms lead to juvenile delinquency. (1.4)
1.0 ─    5. Open classrooms are a communist plot. (1.1)
```

Note: Exact scale values appear in parentheses following each item.

FIGURE 4.4
Attitude scale constructed by Thurstone (1931).

Attitude Toward the Chinese

Try to indicate either agreement or disagreement
for each statement. If you simply cannot decide about
a statement, you may mark it with a question mark.

This is not an examination. There are no right
or wrong answers to these statements. This is simply
a study of people's attitudes toward the Chinese.
Please indicate your own convictions by a check mark
when you agree and by a cross when you disagree.

Put a check mark if you agree with the statement.
Put a cross if you disagree with the statement.

___ 1. I have no particular love or hate for the
        Chinese. (6.5)

___ 2. I dislike the Chinese more every time I see
        one. (10.1)

___ 3. The Chinese are pretty decent. (4.7)

___ 4. Some Chinese traits are admirable, but on the
        whole I don't like them. (7.2)

___ 5. The Chinese are superior to all other races.
        (0.5)

___ 6. The Chinese, as part of the yellow race, are
        inferior to the white race. (8.7)

___ 7. I like the Chinese. (3.5)

___ 8. The more I know about the Chinese the better
        I like them. (2.8)

___ 9. The Chinese are aptly described by the term
        "yellow devils." (11.0)

___ 10. The high-class Chinese are superior to us.
        (1.8)

___ 11. The Chinese are different but not inferior.
        (5.2)

___ 12. I hate the Chinese. (11.5)

___ 13. Chinese parents are unusually devoted to their
        children. (4.1)

___ 14. Although I respect some of their qualities, I
        could never consider a Chinese as a friend. (7.7)

FIGURE 4.4 (continued)

_____ 15. I would rather live in China than any other place in the world. (1.2)

_____ 16. There are no refined or cultured Chinese. (9.7)

_____ 17. The Chinese are no better and no worse than any other people. (6.0)

_____ 18. I think Chinese should be kept out of the United States. (8.4)

_____ 19. I consider it a privilege to associate with Chinese people. (2.2)

_____ 20. The Chinese are inferior in every way. (10.6)

_____ 21. I don't see how anyone could ever like the Chinese. (9.4)

_____ 22. Chinese have a very high sense of honor. (3.0)

_____ 23. I have no desire to know any Chinese. (8.6)

_____ 24. Chinese people have a refinement and depth of feeling that you don't find anywhere else. (1.4)

_____ 25. There is nothing about the Chinese that I like or admire. (9.8)

_____ 26. I'd like to know more Chinese people. (3.9)

Note: Scale values appear in parentheses following each item.

scale values on the two forms. Of course, constructing a second form simply because it's easily done hardly seems an adequate reason for doing it. Only if an alternative form can facilitate one's research is this theoretical advantage a real advantage.

A second advantage that Thurstone scales enjoy over other types of attitude scales is the existence of a "zero" or neutral point. This allows for "absolute" interpretation of scale scores rather than only "relative" interpretation (in which scores have meaning only relative to the scores of other respondents). An attitude score at the neutral point on a Thurstone scale can truly be interpreted as a neutral attitude. In Likert scaling there is *no* clearly neutral point.

In overall comparison with Likert scaling the Thurstone procedure comes off second best, though. Both types of scales, if carefully constructed, can achieve reliability coefficients in the .80s, but Likert scales can often match the reliability of Thurstone scales with slightly fewer items. The biggest drawback of Thurstone scaling, however, is the amount of effort required. The necessity for administration to a group of judges, totally separate from the administration to scale respondents, is enough to tip the balance, for most researchers, in favor of the Likert scaling method.

SUMMARY OF THURSTONE SCALING PROCEDURES

1. Identify the attitudinal object; delimit it quite specifically.

2. Develop a pool of about 50 belief items about the attitudinal object. Try to ensure that these range from extremely unfavorable to extremely favorable toward the attitudinal object. Neutral items must be included.

3. Obtain scale values for all items. These result from averaging (median is preferable to mean) the "favorableness" judgments of 10 or more judges, using a rating form such as is found in Figure 4.1. Make sure judges rate the relative favorableness (positiveness) of each item rather than indicating their own agreement or disagreement.

4. Compute a measure of dispersion of the judges' ratings for each item (e.g., interquartile range, standard deviation, or average deviation). Eliminate items on which the judges don't agree.

5. Select about 20 approximately equidistant items (based on scale values).

6. Randomize their order and print them in an administration form, as found in Figure 4.2.

7. Instruct respondents (those whose attitudes are to be measured) to mark the items with which they agree.

8. Average the scale values of all items marked to obtain an attitude score for each respondent.

5

Guttman Scaling

In 1944 Louis Guttman introduced a scaling procedure designed to produce scales that are strictly unidimensional. When applied to attitude measurement, Guttman scales consist of opinion items similar to those in Likert and Thurstone scales. Guttman scale items are arranged by degree of positiveness or favorableness, just as are Thurstone scale items. What makes Guttman scaling unique is the extreme stress on unidimensionality. A respondent whose score on a Guttman scale places him at a particular point on the attitude continuum *must* agree with *all* items below (less positive than) his own scale position and *must* disagree with *all* items above his scale position. This characteristic of Guttman scaling is called *reproducibility*. Based upon a respondent's scale score, his responses to all scale items are reproducible.

An example will best serve to illustrate this unique characteristic of Guttman scales. Below are five opinion items about abortion, arranged in order of positiveness:

1. Abortion is acceptable under any circumstances.
2. Abortion is an acceptable mechanism for family planning.
3. Abortion is acceptable in cases of rape.
4. Abortion is acceptable if the fetus is found to be seriously malformed.
5. Abortion is acceptable if the mother's life is in danger.

According to the Guttman scaling model, a respondent agreeing with item number 1 should agree with all items below number 1. A respondent who disagrees with item number 1 but agrees with item number 2 should also agree with items 3, 4, 5, and so forth. Whereas in Thurstone scaling items are graduated in favorableness based upon *average* judgments, in Guttman scaling there must be total agreement (among respondents) regarding the ordering of statements. Absolute enforcement of this criterion is virtually impossible in the attitude domain, especially over large numbers of respondents. A statistical *coefficient of reproducibility* is used to determine the extent of adherence to the reproducibility standard in each Guttman scale.

CONSTRUCTING GUTTMAN SCALES

Opinion items thought to be graduated in favorableness toward the attitudinal object are formulated and administered to respondents, generally using a simple "agree"-"disagree" response format. A response matrix of items by respondents is thus generated (see Table 5.1). For each respondent a total scale score is calculated, based upon the number of "agree" responses. For each item, the proportion of respondents making the point-getting ("agree") response is calculated. These figures are listed as marginal statistics in the item response matrix (Table 5.1).

Next, both items and respondents are rearranged in order of magnitude (Table 5.2). The transformed matrix exhibits a triangular pattern of positive item responses characteristic in Guttman scale analysis. This matrix facilitates the identification of items that are identical or nearly identical in "difficulty" and items with inconsistent response patterns, as judged by Guttman scaling criteria. This matrix is also used in the assessment of scale reproducibility.

TESTING FOR REPRODUCIBILITY

Guttman proposed a simple index of scale reproducibility (Rep): the proportion of responses following the prescribed response pattern, or

$$\text{Rep} = 1 - \frac{\text{total number of errors}}{\text{total number of responses}}$$

TABLE 5.1
Response Matrix for Guttman Scale Items

Respondent	Item 1	2	3	4	5	Total
A	1	0	1	0	1	3
B	1	0	1	1	1	4
C	0	1	1	1	1	4
D	0	0	1	0	1	2
E	0	0	0	0	1	1
F	1	0	0	0	1	2
G	1	1	1	1	1	5
H	0	0	0	0	0	0
Proportion	.50	.25	.63	.38	.88	

TABLE 5.2
Guttman Response Matrix Transformed to Triangular
Pattern

	Item					
Respondent	2	4	1	3	5	Total
G	1	1	1	1	1	5
C	1	1	0	1	1	4
B	0	1	1	1	1	4
A	0	0	1	1	1	3
F	0	0	1	0	1	2
D	0	0	0	1	1	2
E	0	0	0	0	1	1
H	0	0	0	0	0	0
Proportion	.25	.38	.50	.63	.88	

The resultant coefficient indicates the proportion of all item responses that are "reproducible" from knowledge of total scale scores, across respondents. Since it is unrealistic to expect attitude (or other affective) scales to be perfectly reproducible, Guttman suggested .90 as the minimum acceptable level of reproducibility.

By Guttman's error-counting method, the data in Table 5.2 would yield a coefficient of reproducibility of .94, with 33 of 35 responses following the prescribed pattern. Guttman would assign one error for the response pattern of respondent C (1 1 0 1 1), maintaining that it "should" be 1 1 1 1 1, and one error for respondent F (0 0 1 0 1), which should be 0 0 1 1 1. Guttman's error-counting procedure, however, has been challenged, and alternate error-counting procedures have been suggested. One of the most popular alternate procedures is that of Goodenough and Edwards (Edwards, 1957). According to this procedure the number of response errors for respondent C would be calculated as two, with the "correct" response pattern being 0 1 1 1 1. Likewise, the pattern for respondent F should be 0 0 0 1 1, also resulting in two errors. The resultant coefficient of reproducibility is .89 (31 ÷ 35). As you can readily see, the method of error counting selected has a dramatic impact upon the resultant coefficient of reproducibility and upon the commensurate judgment of scale quality.

To further confound the interpretation of reproducibility, it has been noted that scale reproducibility is, in part, dependent upon item response distributions, with items of moderate difficulty having the greatest potential for error. Thus scales with an excess of extreme items (items with which most respondents agree, or with which most respondents disagree) will exhibit spuriously high levels of reproducibility.

In order to resolve this difficulty, Edwards (1957) proposed comparing the coefficient of reproducibility with an index of minimum possible reproducibility, based upon the item response distributions. This index he labeled *minimum marginal reproducibility* (MMR). Menzel (1953) noted that *relative* difference between Rep and MMR, rather than *absolute* difference, is the critical comparison. He devised the *coefficient of scalability* as a relative index of this difference.[1]

ASSESSMENT OF GUTTMAN SCALES IN ATTITUDE MEASUREMENT

Without question, the Guttman scaling technique (also known as scalogram analysis, cumulative scaling, and deterministic scaling) results in attitude scales that are more unidimensional than those that result from the Likert or Thurstone techniques. Another way to express this condition is to say that the attitude construct, as operationalized in Guttman scaling, is more narrowly focused than in the other scaling methods. Whether psychological constructs should be broadly or narrowly defined is a perennial issue among social scientists. When constructs are narrowly defined, scale scores have a very precise psychological interpretation. This facilitates comparison of individual respondents. In Guttman scaling, for instance, the exact pattern of beliefs of each scale respondent, within the domain of the scale's assessment, is known from his total scale score.

In scales measuring broader constructs, scale scores have a less precise meaning. In Likert scaling, for instance, two respondents can achieve the same scale score through substantially different patterns of agreeing and disagreeing with scale items. Can we truly conclude that they have the same attitude?

The trade-off is that when constructs are very narrowly defined—and measured—more constructs are required to explain a particular domain of the psychological universe. There are many belief and opinion items about abortion that could be incorporated into a Likert or Thurstone scale but are not eligible for the sample Guttman scale presented at the beginning of this chapter (e.g., "Abortion should be discouraged;" "The increase in abortion indicates deterioration of our country's moral fiber;" "Abortion is a viable solution to the problem of overpopulation;" "Abortion is murder;" "I would vote for a pro-choice candidate"). These statements represent por-

---

[1]See the descriptions of the SPSS GUTTMAN SCALE and SAS GUTTMAN PROCEDURE computer programs in Appendix B.

tions of the attitude domain that *cannot* be covered by this Guttman scale. Using Guttman scaling, the only means of capturing these other portions of the attitude toward abortion domain is to construct more scales, one for each "dimension."

The other limitations of Guttman scaling are the somewhat technical nature of the scaling process and the uncertainty of the quality of any particular Guttman scale due to the alternate procedures for counting errors and the alternate methods of interpreting the coefficient of reproducibility.

For more detailed descriptions of procedures for constructing and evaluating Guttman scales see Guttman (1944), Edwards (1957), and Gordon (1977).

6
The Semantic Differential

As was explained in Chapter 1, the semantic differential, developed by Charles Osgood and his associates, was not originally designed for the purpose of attitude measurement. Osgood was studying the nature of meaning. He believed that the thousands of adjectives that we use to describe the world around us have considerable connotative overlap. Using a statistical technique called factor analysis, he attempted to identify the underlying dimensions of meaning. He found that a large proportion of all meaning can be accounted for with three cognitive dimensions: evaluation, potency, and activity.

The semantic differential is Osgood's instrument for measuring the extent to which respondents attribute each of the several meaning dimensions to particular objects. Pairs of opposite adjectives that are highly representative of the dimension(s) to be measured serve as "items." Respondents indicate the extent to which each adjective (or its paired opposite) describes the object.

Figure 6.1 is an example of a semantic differential designed to measure the three major dimensions of meaning found by Osgood. This figure illustrates the commonly used semantic differential administrative format. (The meaning dimension represented by each adjective pair is indicated for instructional purposes; these are not so identified for respondents.) Additional dimensions of meaning can be measured by including adjective pairs representative of those dimensions in the instrument. Adjective pairs are normally separated by seven response categories representing equal units along the adjective-opposites continua. A common practice is to randomly alter the "direction" of the adjective continua (e.g., in Figure 6.1 *valuable* and *clean*, both connoting positive evaluation, appear on the left ends of their respective continua: *good* and *fair*, also connoting positive evaluation, appear on the right ends of their continua). This convention is designed to overcome response sets that could adversely affect the validity of the instrument. Response sets are discussed in greater detail in Chapter 7.

FIGURE 6.1
Sample semantic differential designed to measure three
dimensions of meaning.

My Spouse

valuable	___:___:___:___:___:___:___	worthless
clean	___:___:___:___:___:___:___	dirty
bad	___:___:___:___:___:___:___	good
unfair	___:___:___:___:___:___:___	fair
large	___:___:___:___:___:___:___	small
strong	___:___:___:___:___:___:___	weak
deep	___:___:___:___:___:___:___	shallow
fast	___:___:___:___:___:___:___	slow
active	___:___:___:___:___:___:___	passive
hot	___:___:___:___:___:___:___	cold

Note: The first four adjective pairs measure the
evaluation dimension; the next three measure potency;
and the last three measure activity.

USE IN ATTITUDE MEASUREMENT

For purposes of attitude measurement a special form of the semantic differential, consisting entirely of adjective pairs representing the *evaluation* dimension, is constructed. Figure 6.2 lists adjective pairs that Osgood found to "load" highly on the evaluation dimension in his factor analyses.

Usually a few adjective pairs are sufficient to produce a scale with high internal consistency. Selected adjective pairs will not work equally well, though, across attitudinal objects. The adjective pair *high-low*, for example, normally contains a large proportion of evaluative meaning. But when this adjective pair is used with reference to the attitudinal object "marijuana," it may *not* connote evaluation. Likewise, a Volkswagen "Beetle" owner and devotee may rate VW Beetle toward the *ugly* end of a *beautiful-ugly* continuum, with no negative evaluation intended.

The safe course is to select several (perhaps six or seven) adjective pairs

FIGURE 6.2
Adjective pairs found to be high in the evaluation
dimension of meaning.

good-bad	kind-cruel
nice-awful	honest-dishonest
beautiful-ugly	fair-unfair
pleasant-unpleasant	high-low
clean-dirty	fragrant-foul
sweet-sour	successful-unsuccessful
sacred-profane	reputable-disreputable
valuable-worthless	tasteful-distasteful

Source: Osgood et al. (1957), p. 37.

initially, perform an item analysis[1] (just as in Likert scaling), and eliminate the weaker items. Figure 6.3 is an example of a semantic differential consisting of nine potentially evaluative adjective pairs designed to measure attitudes toward marijuana. Administered to a group of 24 college students, the scale had an internal consistency (alpha) coefficient of .86. When the four adjective pairs with the lowest correlations with total scale score (*ugly-beautiful, clean-dirty, useless-valuable,* and *high-low*) were eliminated, leaving a five-item scale, the alpha increased to .95. (The *high-low* adjective pair, incidentally, correlated -.28 with the total score from the nine-item scale.)

In scoring the semantic differential, each item (adjective pair) can contribute from one to seven points to the total score, the most positive response receiving a 7 and the most negative a 1. Thus, a semantic differential consisting of five pairs of evaluative adjectives would have a score range from 5 to 35.

STRENGTHS AND WEAKNESSES OF THE SEMANTIC DIFFERENTIAL

The semantic differential has much to recommend it as a self-report attitude-measurement technique. It is relatively easy to construct, it is

---

[1]See the descriptions of the SPSS RELIABILITY and EDSTAT TESTAT computer programs in Appendix B.

FIGURE 6.3
Osgood's semantic differential measuring attitude toward
marijuana.

Check (✓) the position between each adjective pair
which best describes the meaning of <u>marijuana</u> to you.

MARIJUANA

ugly	___:___:___:___:___:___:___	beautiful
positive	___:___:___:___:___:___:___	negative
kind	___:___:___:___:___:___:___	cruel
bad	___:___:___:___:___:___:___	good
clean	___:___:___:___:___:___:___	dirty
useless	___:___:___:___:___:___:___	valuable
wonderful	___:___:___:___:___:___:___	terrible
unpleasant	___:___:___:___:___:___:___	pleasant
high	___:___:___:___:___:___:___	low

<u>Note:</u> All adjective pairs measure the <u>evaluation</u>
dimension of meaning.

short and thus quick to administer, and it is usually highly reliable. (Test-retest reliabilities and internal-consistency coefficients around .90 are common for well-constructed semantic differential scales used to measure the evaluative dimension.) Furthermore, semantic differential attitude-scale scores typically correlate very highly with scores from Likert and Thurstone attitude scales. The semantic differential does have several drawbacks, though. Administration rapport is sometimes a problem. Respondents who insist on a literal interpretation will sometimes balk at applying some adjective pairs to some attitudinal objects ("What do you mean, how *dirty* or *clean* is my mother? I'm not going to mark anything on that item"). As you can see, it's critical to impress on respondents the importance, for meaningful measurement, of answering all items—even if they experience a small amount of psychological discomfort in the process. It might help to tell them that some items will be discarded after statistical analysis.

A second problem is in the realm of validity. Respondents can slant their attitude-scale scores at will. Semantic differential attitude scales are very blatant or "transparent" in their purpose. It is relatively easy for respondents to figure out what is being measured. This is true, to some extent, with Likert, Thurstone, and Guttman scales, but of the four, the semantic differential comes closest to simply asking respondents, "What is your attitude toward object x?" or "How positively (negatively) do you feel about object x?" Methods of combating such (conscious or unconscious) biasing of responses are discussed in Chapter 7.

Another possible problem in using the semantic differential for attitude measurement is failing to isolate the evaluative dimension. It should be clear from the above discussion that the measurement of meaning and the measurement of attitude are not synonymous. Attitude, or evaluation, is only one dimension of meaning. But sometimes researchers or evaluators in a hurry to select an attitude-measurement instrument find and use an instrument such as is shown in Figure 6.1 when they should be using one such as in Figure 6.3. When items measuring two or more dimensions of meaning are combined in a single scale score, the meaning of that score is unclear. It should most certainly *not* be characterized as a measure of attitude.

Even worse, some researchers bring together a conglomeration of adjective-opposite pairs in a semantic differential format, with no particular psychological construct in mind at all, and call it attitude measurement. Their mistake is to associate the *attitude* label with the semantic differential instrumentation format. If the items are not working together to measure a particular psychological variable, not only is this not attitude measurement, it is not the measurement of *any* psychological trait.

7
Reliability and Validity
of Attitude Measures

Reliability and validity are the benchmark criteria for assessing the quality of all measurement devices and procedures. If a measurement instrument is *valid*, it is measuring the right thing—what it is supposed to be measuring. If it is *reliable*, its measurement is consistent and accurate, rather than random. In the study of social and psychological phenomena, the elements of measurement are abstract constructs (concepts) such as attitudes, values, and personality traits. Unlike the measurement of physical traits or conditions such as height, weight, and temperature, psychological traits cannot be seen or felt. Nor can they be measured directly. They must be inferred from people's beliefs and behaviors. This measurement process is extremely prone to error. For this reason psychometric and sociometric researchers must take particular care to maximize the quality (the reliability and validity) of their measurement instruments and procedures.

This chapter will discuss the commonly used methods for assessing the reliability and validity of psychological measurement instruments. Since many of these methods use the statistical technique of *correlation*, it will be useful to review the important characteristics of the correlation statistic before proceeding farther.

Correlation was introduced in Chapter 2 as a statistical device for studying the relationship of each item in an attitude scale to scores on the total scale (item discrimination). You will remember that a correlation coefficient of 1.00 indicates a perfect, positive relationship between two variables, and a zero correlation (.00) indicates no relationship at all. Thus a reliability (correlation) coefficient of 1.00 indicates perfect reliability, whereas a reliability coefficient of .00 indicates no reliability whatsoever (essentially random scoring). Likewise, validity coefficients of 1.00 and .00 indicate, respectively, total or perfect validity and no validity.

Never do we see either reliability or validity coefficients of 1.00, however. These qualities exist on continua of more or less. A well-constructed attitude scale, for instance, may have a reliability coefficient of .80 or even .90. A less well-constructed scale may have a reliability only in the .50s or .60s. Validity can range anywhere from .00 to about as high as the reliability coefficient (more about the interrelationship of reliability and validity later in this chapter). In reality, validity coefficients of psychological measures seldom even approach 1.00 and frequently are below .50. Thus it is inappropriate to conclude that a particular test is valid or not valid or is reliable or not reliable. Rather, each test or scale has *some degree* of reliability and of validity. In fact, as we shall see shortly, reliability and validity coefficients for a particular test may vary from situation to situation.

RELIABILITY-ESTIMATION PROCEDURES

If a measurement instrument produces highly reliable scores, then each respondent's score can be believed; it can be depended upon in drawing conclusions and making decisions; it is trustworthy. This is much the same meaning that the word *reliability* has in common parlance—when applied to friends, cars, or employees. With high reliability, attitude-scale scores of individuals can safely be compared and can legitimately be correlated with other measures. If a measurement instrument has low reliability, neither of these statistical uses is acceptable. Psychological measurement, as we have learned, is never perfectly reliable. This is largely due to the inferential process required in "measuring" hypothetical constructs through responses to test items (or some other aspect of testee behavior). We might even go so far as to say that every score on a psychological measure is likely to be *wrong*. With careful scale-construction techniques, though, we can ensure that the measurement error, on the average, is not more than a few points. The reliability statistic is designed to estimate the amount of error present in psychological test scores. In fact, reliability coefficients indicate the proportion of the total variance in test scores that is legitimate, or "true" score variance. A test with a reliability coefficient of .80 thus has 80 percent true score variance and 20 percent error variance.

There are four procedures for calculating the reliability of a psychological measure, such as an attitude scale: test-retest, alternate forms, split-half, and internal consistency. While each procedure is distinct, there are some conceptual similarities across procedures.

Test-Retest

If a person is measured twice with the same psychological test or scale, he ought to receive the same score. In the test-retest procedure an attitude scale is administered twice to the same group of people. Scores from the first testing are correlated with scores from the second testing. The resulting correlation coefficient is called a reliability coefficient. If high scorers on the first testing score high on the retest, average scorers score average, and low scorers score low, the test is judged substantially reliable. As you can see, however, retest scores may legitimately differ from the original scores because of a real change in attitude (or achievement, or whatever trait is being measured) between testings. The retest scores may also be affected by remembering the items and responses made in the first testing. To overcome these problems it is desirable that the time between testings be long enough for testees to forget the details of the first testing but short enough so that little or no real change in attitude occurs between the testings. A few weeks often turns out to be a good compromise.

Alternate Forms

An alternate form of a test or scale is an equivalent test or scale that measures the same content as the original form but with different items. Administering both forms to the same group of people can be a mechanism for estimating their reliabilities. As in the test-retest procedure, the scores from the two testings (in this case the two forms) are correlated to obtain a reliability coefficient. The alternate-forms procedure has an advantage over the test-retest procedure in that test takers' recall of items and responses from the first testing has no influence on scores in the second testing because the items are different. The second form may be administered immediately after the first form, thus also overcoming the problem of real change between testings; or it can be administered after a time interval. The different content in the items of alternate forms, though, almost inevitably causes the two sets of scores to be somewhat different. In fact, the alternate-forms reliability-estimation procedure tends to produce the most conservative (lowest) reliability estimates of the four procedures—especially if there is also a substantial time lag between testings.

Split-Half

Both the test-retest and the alternate-forms procedures require two test administrations. The split-half procedure requires only a single administration. Conceptually, the split-half procedure is somewhat similar to the alternate-forms procedure. First the test or scale is administered to a group of people. The test items are then divided, for purposes of scoring, into two half-length tests. Each respondent thus receives two scores, one for each half-test. As in the previously described procedures, these two sets of scores are correlated. But this correlation coefficient indicates only the reliability of the half-length tests. Since correlation is directly associated with variance (spread of scores), and variance is directly associated with test length, a full-length test would be expected to have somewhat higher reliability than a half-length test. Two psychometric statisticians, Charles Spearman and William Brown, have worked out a formula that estimates the reliability of the full-length test based on the reliability of the half-length tests. Called the "Spearman-Brown formula for doubled length" or the "Spearman-Brown prophecy formula," it is as follows:

$$\text{Reliability of whole test} = \frac{2 \times \text{reliability of half test}}{1 + \text{reliability of half test}}$$

Thus, for example, if the half-length tests intercorrelate .60, the reliability of the whole test equals $1.20 \div 1.60$, or .75.

The one remaining question in implementing the split-half procedure is: How do we split the test into halves? There are, of course, many possible ways to divide the test items into halves. Keeping in mind that the halves are to serve much as alternate forms, an effort should be made to match the two half-length tests in content, item type, item difficulty, and any other item characteristics that might affect responses. One of the simplest procedures, yet one that will effectively balance the content and difficulty of the halves, is the "odd-even" procedure: scoring odd-numbered items in one half and even-numbered items in the other.

Split-half reliability is a popular method for reliability estimation because it is easy to understand and easy to carry out and because it requires only a single test administration. The odd-even procedure is usually the item-splitting method of choice. (This procedure cannot easily be applied to the Thurstone scaling method because the scoring of items is based on their favorableness values and because each respondent is expected to agree with only a few Thurstone scale items.)

Internal Consistency

Internal consistency differs somewhat from the other reliability-estimation procedures. A procedural difference is that the correlation statistic is not used directly; there are not two sets of scores that are intercorrelated. A conceptual difference is that an internal-consistency coefficient tells us about similarity in measurement across items rather than stability over time or across forms. In much the same way as the split-half procedure is an index of consistency between *halves*, so the internal-consistency procedure is an index of *interitem* consistency.

The most well-known internal-consistency formulas are the Kuder-

Richardson formula 20 (K-R 20) and the Cronbach alpha (α) (Kuder and Richardson, 1937; Cronbach, 1951). K-R 20 is for use with tests having dichotomously scored items, such as aptitude tests (right or wrong), or affective scales with items having only two response categories (e.g., "agree"-"disagree") that are scored "1" and "0." Tests with items scored along a continuum, such as Likert scale attitude items (scored 1 through 5), require the use of alpha. (Actually, alpha is a more general form of K-R 20.) The alpha formula is as follows:

$$\text{alpha} = \left(\frac{k}{k-1}\right)\left(1 - \frac{\Sigma\, s_i^2}{s_t^2}\right)$$

where: k = number of test items
  s_t^2 = variance[1] of total test scores
  Σ = sum (for all test items)
  s_i^2 = variance of responses to a test item

The element "$k \div (k - 1)$" in the above formula will always be greater than 1.00. If the test is even moderate in length, though, this ratio will be very close to 1.00 (e.g., $20 \div 19 = 1.05$) and thus will have little impact on the resulting statistic (alpha).

The other element in the formula, "$1 - (\Sigma s_i^2 \div s_t^2)$," is basically a ratio of test score variance to the summed variance of all test items. Alpha becomes larger or smaller as the ratio of Σs_i^2 to s_t^2 changes. If we can understand what condition of test items will cause s_t^2 to be large relative to Σs_i^2 we will have captured the essence of the alpha reliability formula.

The key to this question is the intercorrelation of test items. When test items are substantially intercorrelated (i.e., are working together in effecting similar discrimination among respondents), s_t^2 will be considerably larger than when test items are not intercorrelated. When the items are *not* intercorrelated, the discrimination caused by each item is independent of the discrimination caused by all other items. The summed item variance (Σs_i^2), by comparison, will not be affected by the intercorrelation of items.

---

[1]*Variance*, both for total test scores and for individual item responses, is an index of spread or dispersion. Its formula is

$$s2 = \frac{\Sigma\,(X - \bar{X})^2}{N}$$

where: X = raw score
  $\bar{X}$ = mean (of all the raw scores)
  Σ = sum (of all squared raw score deviations from the mean)
  N = number of raw scores

Thus the alpha coefficient will be larger (i.e., closer to 1.00) when the test items are intercorrelated. This is the meaning of "internal-consistency" reliability.

Another way to understand alpha is in relation to the split-half procedure. The alpha coefficient is exactly the same as the mean of all possible split-half coefficients (many different split-half coefficients would result from many different splits). In effect, alpha treats each *item* as an alternate test form and establishes the consistency of measurement across forms. In this model, the average of all item intercorrelations is considered the average *item* reliability. A more general form of the Spearman-Brown prophecy formula can then be used to estimate the reliability of all items combined. Internal-consistency reliability-estimation procedures are particularly relevant for tests measuring psychological constructs (such as attitudes, values, and personality traits). In these instances it is important for all items to be measuring the same underlying variable (the psychological construct). All items must discriminate similarly among test takers. Consequently, the items should intercorrelate moderately. For some other kinds of tests, internal consistency is less important (e.g., achievement tests, prediction tests, and skill tests).

It is important to understand that none of these reliability-estimation procedures is the "right" one or even the best one. They are referred to as reliability-*estimation* procedures rather than reliability-*computation* procedures because each procedure is plagued with a source of error that cannot be totally eliminated. Furthermore, while the four reliability models have some conceptual similarity, they also have considerable conceptual distinctiveness. The meaning of high test-retest reliability, for example, is very different from the meaning of high internal-consistency reliability. Whenever a reliability coefficient is reported, it is important to indicate which of the procedures was used. In fact, applying more than one of the procedures to a particular test will enrich understanding of the test's measurement qualities.

VALIDATION PROCEDURES

There are three major validity models that may be applied to attitude scales and other psychological measures: content validity, predictive validity, and construct validity.

Content Validity

The content-validity model was developed in the realm of achievement testing, and its applicability is greatest in that realm. First, the entire universe of content to be measured is outlined. The relative importance of each content subarea is established, and test items are written or selected to reflect this content emphasis. In effect, the test items sample the content universe to be measured.

This validity model applies less well to the measurement of affective traits. The difficulty lies in circumscribing the "universe" of a psychological construct. What, for example, is the universe for the construct *attitude toward abortion?* If an attitude is the sum of positive and negative affect denoted or connoted in all of a person's beliefs (opinions) about the attitudinal object, we can *approximate* the content-validity model by including a wide variety of positive and negative opinion statements about the attitudinal object in our scale. Ultimately, however, this validity model cannot stand alone in the validation of psychological scales.

There is no statistical index of content validity. The process must simply be documented.

Predictive Validity

Predictive validity is the extent to which a test accurately predicts a criterion—for example, the extent to which a scholastic achievement test predicts subsequent school performance. The statistical index of predictive validity is the correlation between the predictor and the criterion. The predictive validity of an attitude measure is its correlation with a criterion behavior.

During the early developmental years of psychometric psychology there was great hope and anticipation that psychological tests, both cognitive and affective, would provide the basis for an exact science of predicting human behavior. Attitude scales, in particular, were expected to serve expertly in this capacity. Unfortunately, it was not to be so. The social psychological literature is full of studies in which an attitude measure (frequently a Likert, Thurstone, or semantic differential scale) is used to predict a particular behavior. These predictions vary in success from zero to moderately good. But the average predictability is low.

There are three major reasons for the lack of predictive success of attitude measures: (1) The reliability of the attitude measures used in these studies is sometimes quite low. (2) People don't always behave in accord with their attitudes. (3) There is sometimes dissimilarity in the attitudinal and behavioral objects studied.

Reliability of the Attitude Measure. Reliability is a precondition for validity. If an instrument is not measuring *anything* consistently (reliability), then it can't possibly be measuring the *right* thing (validity). The upper limit for a validity coefficient is expressed as follows:

$$validity \leq \sqrt{reliability}$$

This formula says that the validity coefficient can be equal to or less than (never greater than) the square root of the reliability coefficient. A scale with a reliability of .81 can have a validity of .90. A scale with a reliability of .49 can have a validity of .70. It should be noted that high reliability is no guarantee of high validity. A highly reliable measure can have a validity of .00.

We have learned that well-constructed attitude scales exhibit reliability coefficients in the .80s or even in the .90s. This is by no means perfect reliability, but it is far better than random assignment of scores—certainly not low enough to explain the generally low correlations with behavioral measures. Unfortunately, studies addressing this prediction issue do not always use high-quality measures of attitude. Some use attitude scales containing only a few items. Some scales have ambiguous items. In many predictive-validity studies the reliability of the attitude measure is not mentioned. Some use only a single question as an index of attitude. In many studies reporting low relationships between attitude measures and behavior, the reliability of the predictive (attitude) measure is unacceptably low.

Behavior Not in Accord with Attitude. A causal model, with attitude toward an object causing behaviors toward the object, is a basically correct model. But attitude is only one of many causes of behavior. A variety of values, other attitudes, and situational variables frequently cause people to behave in opposition to their attitudes. A person may buy a particular video cassette recorder that is not his first choice because he can't afford the one he really wants. Other products and services that he also likes or needs compete for his finite resources. He may even go through life without a video recorder because of these conflicting demands. Or an individual may vacation at the ocean though she prefers the mountains because her friends are vacationing at the ocean and she wants to vacation with them. Even in making major life decisions people sometimes compromise their attitudinal preferences. Someone may take a job that she doesn't like because there are no other jobs available. Or a person may buy a two-story house though he prefers a one-story house because his wife wants a two-story house. Examples are infinite.

Recently I found myself in a situation where two of my attitudinal positions were in direct conflict. I own a modest number of shares of stock in our local power company. My primary motivation is to earn a couple of hundred dollars in untaxed dividends each year. As a result I have a positive attitude toward the power company and hope it prospers financially.

(Besides, I grew up in an era when public utilities were considered to be among the good guys.) I am also a member of the Sierra Club. I believe I have more than an average concern for the welfare of Mother Nature, and the Sierra Club supports this attitudinal position. Congress was considering legislation to reduce the stringency of air pollution standards. The power company sent me letters telling me to support the legislation because it was in the best interest of my financial security (and wouldn't really hurt anyone). The Sierra Club sent me letters urging me to combat the legislation because it was not in the best interests of humanity (which, of course, includes Bambi, Thumper, and my kids). Either behavior on my part would have been in consort with one of my attitudinal positions but in opposition to another.[2]

Some social scientists have used the term *situational variables* to explain the discrepancies between attitude and overt behavior toward an attitudinal object. Their thesis is that situational variables, such as social pressures, actual behavioral options, economic circumstances, and the effects of competing values and conflicting attitudes, frequently cause people to act in violation of their attitudinal preferences. One study that graphically establishes the effect of situational variables on behavior was conducted by Wicker (1971). He predicted three behaviors: frequency of church attendance, monetary contributions to church, and participation in church activities. As predictors he used (1) a scale measuring attitude toward the church, (2) a measure of perceived consequences of the criterion behaviors (e.g., "Attending church sets a good example for one's children"), (3) a measure of subjects' evaluation of the behaviors, and (4) a measure of judged influence of extraneous events on the criterion behaviors (e.g., "What would be the effect on your church attendance if you had weekend guests who did not regularly attend church?" "How would your monetary contributions be affected if the congregation voted to spend funds on a project of which you disapproved?"). In the prediction of all three behaviors, the judged influence of extraneous events correlated more highly with the criterion behaviors (average $r = .37$) than did the attitude toward the church measure (average $r = .21$).

In some instances people are even *coerced* to act in opposition to their attitudes. Incarcerated populations (e.g., prisoners or mental patients) supply extreme examples of behaviors that don't conform to attitudes. But numerous examples exist in everyday life. Many a small child has eaten

---

[2]Since then my power company stock has become nearly worthless owing to the unwise investment of billions of dollars in a now-abandoned nuclear power plant. In addition, I have allowed my Sierra Club membership to lapse because of some too-radical positions taken by that organization. My attitudinal conflict has disappeared, but neither the financial health of my "estate" nor the environmental health of our planet has benefited in the process.

vegetables he didn't like because his parents thought they were good for him. Sometimes husbands attend parties that they don't enjoy because their wives require them to attend. And wives go on fishing vacations they don't like because their husbands insist. Congressional representatives vote for legislation they don't believe in because of pressure from powerful lobby groups. And soldiers kill fellow human beings because their government requires them to. In such instances it is possible that the attitude measure is actually a *better* index of "real" attitude than is the behavior.

But the focus of this discussion is not on comparing one index of attitude with another. In the predictive model the focus is on predicting behavior. Most of the studies on behavior prediction from attitude measures have focused on a single, specific behavior, such as voting Democratic in a particular election, contributing money to a lobby group, or attending church in a particular week. It seems likely that predictive success would be better if *patterns of behavior* toward an attitudinal object, rather than isolated behaviors, were predicted. I like my parents and my brothers a great deal (attitude), but I didn't visit them last year (single behavior). My attitude, in this case, does not predict my behavior. (My family, incidentally, lives 2,000 miles away.) I do write to them occasionally, telephone them often, invite them to visit me, send them gifts, and talk fondly about them often (behavior pattern). If all of these behaviors were measured, a good index of my attitude would emerge. Conversely, my attitude toward my family, as measured by an attitude scale, would coincide with my *pattern* of behavior toward them (attitude would predict behavior.)

A research study that clearly supports this thesis (that attitude measures predict *behavior patterns* better than they predict *isolated behaviors*) was reported by Tittle and Hill (1967). These researchers constructed scales of varying length, using several methods (Likert, Thurstone, and Guttman), that measured attitude toward personal participation in political activities. They also constructed scales of varying length measuring behaviors toward this attitudinal object. Their results were quite convincing. The relationships between attitude-scale scores and "behavior-scale" scores were directly proportional to the number of behaviors measured. Tittle and Hill also analyzed the results of 15 other studies in which the relationship of overt behavior to measured attitude was examined. They paid particular attention to whether a single act of behavior or a *pattern* of behavioral acts toward the object served as the criterion. They discovered that consistently higher relationships between attitude and behavior occurred when behavioral patterns were predicted than when single acts were predicted. These researchers also noted that predictive validity tended to be greater when behavioral criteria involved normal (usual) life behavioral choices rather than atypical or contrived experimental behaviors.

If accurate prediction of a single behavior is truly the research goal (rather than accurately measuring attitude, or predicting a behavioral syndrome), then even the best of attitude measures cannot be expected to get the job done. Each behavior is caused by a complex interaction of attitudes, values, and situational variables. These must all be entered into the prediction equation in order for accurate prediction of a single behavior to result.

Dissimilarity of Attitudinal and Behavioral Objects.   In what is probably the most often cited study exemplifying the low relationship between attitude and behavior, a sociologist, Richard LaPiere, traveled throughout the United States with a young Chinese couple. LaPiere (1934) noted the behavior toward the Chinese couple of personnel at auto camps, tourist homes, and hotels where the trio stayed. In only one instance were they not hospitably received. Several months later LaPiere sent a letter to each establishment visited, asking them, "Will you accept members of the Chinese race as guests in your establishment?" In over 90 percent of the 128 responses the answer was "No." Response to LaPiere's letter was considered a measure of attitude; actual treatment of the couple, the behavior.

There are several very serious flaws in this study, not the least of which is the uncertainty that the respondents to the letter were the same individuals as the clerks and proprietors who actually served the trio. But for now the point is that there was probably a discrepancy between the attitudinal object and the behavioral object. The behavioral object was a young, well-groomed Chinese couple accompanied by a well-dressed Caucasian. These were the people to whom the hotel and motel personnel actually responded and whom they chose to treat hospitably or not. The attitudinal object was whatever generalized (stereotypic) image came to mind in reference to the word *Chinese* appearing in LaPiere's letter. The Chinese best known to many Americans in the early part of this century were "illiterate" Chinese coolies who served as railroad laborers and in other laboring and service jobs. (This study also exemplifies the measurement of attitude with a single item.)

The problem of behavioral objects that are different from attitudinal objects is fairly common in studies attempting to predict behavior. A person with a very positive attitude toward education may believe that all children should be required to attend school, that the government should allocate more money for education, that more educational programs should be shown on television, that educated people make better citizens, that wars would be reduced if people throughout the world were educated, and that the school year should be lengthened. But *he* may decide not to attend college. In this instance the attitudinal object (education) is very general, whereas the behavior (not attending college) is very specific. The attitudinal beliefs have referred to a variety of presumed social consequences, whereas the behavioral decision is based upon presumed personal consequences. The attitudinal beliefs focus primarily on education at the elementary and secondary school levels, whereas the behavior regards college-level education. Better success in predicting college-attending behavior, for this individual, would doubtless result from measuring attitude toward *college* education and from an attitude scale that focused on *specific* and *personal* consequences than on general and social consequences of education.

A number of researchers have suggested that predictability of behavior from attitude measures can be increased by focusing on *attitudinal objects more specific to the behaviors.* In one study to illustrate this principle Wicker and Pomazal (1971) asked college students to volunteer as subjects in a psychological experiment. They attempted to predict volunteering behavior from each of two attitudinal scales that had been previously administered. One scale measured attitude toward scientific research. The other measured attitude toward participation in a psychological experiment. The more specific measure (attitude toward participation in a psychological experiment) proved to be the better predictor. Likewise, Rokeach and Kliejunas (1972) demonstrated that class-cutting behavior among college students could be predicted much more accurately from subjects' ratings of the importance of attending class (which Rokeach called "attitude toward the situation") than from a measure of attitude toward the instructor.

Martin Fishbein and Icek Ajzen have recently developed a model for the prediction of behavior within the realm of attitude theory. These scientists believe that a behavior can be predicted quite well from a measure of a person's *intention* to perform (or not to perform) that behavior ("Do you intend to vote in the forthcoming election?"). Further, they specify that the closer the intention measurement is to the time of the behavior, the better will be the prediction (Fishbein and Ajzen, 1975). While these may not seem like very profound insights, they have, up until now, been largely ignored by social scientists in their quest to prove that attitudes predict behaviors.

Fishbein and Ajzen go on to explain the origins of *intention* in terms of subjects' *attitude toward the behavior* ("My voting in the forthcoming election is important/good/desirable") and in terms of situational variables that (may) interfere with the execution of one's intention. These they call *subjective norms.* In 1980 these researchers published a book of research applications, in which they convincingly demonstrated the viability of their theory (Ajzen and Fishbein, 1980). From the perspective of the present volume it must be noted, however, that the Fishbein-Ajzen model relates only indirectly to the validation of attitude measures as we have studied them. While their theory does require the measurement of *attitude toward (a particular) behavior* toward the attitudinal object, it makes no direct use of the more traditional conceptualization and measurement of *attitudes toward objects, persons, institutions, and ideas.*

Summary. It must be concluded that attitude measures are not always good predictors of behavior. Conversely, it must be concluded that behaviors are not always good indicators of attitude. If an attitude measure is found not to correlate highly with an index of behavior toward a particular object, it is appropriate to question the reliability and the validity of the attitude measure. It is equally appropriate to question the reliability and validity of the behavioral measure. In some instances it will be found that the attitude measure is a more valid measure of attitude toward an object than is the index of behavior.

The predictive validity of an attitude measure can be optimized if careful attention is given to each component of the predictive paradigm:

1. The attitude measure must have high reliability. This can be accomplished with a well-constructed attitude scale.
2. The criterion measure (behavior index) must also be highly reliable. Again, a multi-item index, such as a scale measuring a pattern of behaviors, is better than a measure of a single overt act.
3. The object of the attitudinal measure and the object of behavior must be identical.
4. Situational variables, which mitigate the attitude-behavior relationship, must be taken into consideration.

Construct Validity

In the predictive-validity model the focus is on the criterion: behavior. Attitude measures serve only as a means for predicting this criterion. If an attitude measure does not predict behavior, it is, by definition, not valid. The question of how well the attitude measure measures attitude is simply not addressed in the predictive-validity model. (Of course, if one maintains that behavior is the "real" or "ultimate" index of attitude, then a lack of predictive validity would also be interpreted as a lack of attitude measurement.)

Unlike the predictive-validity model, construct validity considers attitude to be a legitimate and important entity in its own right, regardless of correlations with overt behavior. Attitude, like all other psychological constructs (such as values, personality traits, and intelligence) is an idealized abstraction that is subject to scientific study and can be measured through inferences about people's beliefs and behaviors (often the behaviors are responses to test items).

The construct-validity model requires a *theory of the construct* under study. A concise definition of the construct is required. Then a series of hypotheses is generated specifying the construct's believed association with each of a variety of social, democratic, and other psychological variables. Construct validity is supported to the extent that these hypotheses are verified. They are called validity hypotheses. Validity hypotheses can be classified into several procedural categories that constitute the empirical base for the construct-validity model. The major procedural categories are explained in the remainder of this section.

Known-Group Difference.   In the known-group difference procedure two groups of people are identified: one "known" to hold positive attitudes toward the attitudinal object and one "known" to hold negative attitudes. The attitude measure being validated is administered to both groups. If the mean score for the positive group is substantially higher than the mean score for the negative group, we have data supporting the validity of the attitude scale. For instance, a group of Republicans and a group of Democrats could be administered a scale presumed to measure attitude toward social welfare. The validity hypothesis might read like this: "If the attitude scale is measuring what it is purported to measure (attitude toward social welfare), then Democrats will score higher than Republicans." Note that this procedure produces no validity coefficient. A statistical test of mean difference supplies the validity evidence.

Correlation with Measures of Similar Constructs.   A scale measuring attitude toward social welfare could be correlated with scales measuring equality value, altruism value, attitude toward the poor, or attitude toward socialized medicine. Since these are similar constructs, moderate to high correlations would be required to support construct validity. Correlations with less-related constructs should be low to moderate but must still be positive. Variables that might be hypothesized to be *somewhat* but not highly related to attitude toward social welfare include need to nurture and political liberalism.

This procedural model is very like the predictive-validity model. A correlation coefficient with a similar construct can also be called a validity coefficient but can only be expected to be as high as the "other construct" is similar to the construct of the scale being validated. Unlike predictive validity, though, the other construct would not necessarily qualify as a "criterion." This type of construct validity is sometimes called convergent validity.

Correlation with Unrelated and Dissimilar Constructs. A scale measuring attitude toward social welfare would be expected to correlate zero or nearly zero with measures of unrelated constructs (e.g., intelligence, extroversion, attitude toward pistachio ice cream, and valuing salvation) and negatively with measures of dissimilar constructs (e.g., independence value, competition value, attitude toward corporate executives, and yearly income).

You may be thinking that this is scant evidence of validity. And, of course, the fact that the attitude-toward-social-welfare scale does not correlate with a measure of extroversion does not *prove* that it is measuring attitude toward social welfare. But the lack of correlation with an unrelated construct does *support* the validity of our scale. We certainly would be surprised (and disappointed) if our scale correlated highly with a measure of extroversion or attitude toward pistachio ice cream. In fact, that would constitute *negative* validity evidence. In effect we are saying that data that fail to support invalidity are support for validity. Granted, this is a small morsel of validity evidence. In general, though, that's the way construct validity works. Evidence for validity comes in small pieces, with no single piece of evidence being sufficient to "prove" validity. I like to equate construct validation with the process of building a stone wall. Each stone is analogous to a piece of construct-validity data. The stones come in different sizes (with correlations of zero with unrelated constructs constituting very small stones, indeed). Many stones are needed to build a strong wall.

Internal Consistency. The internal-consistency concept was discussed in the reliability section. Now we will see that it can also supply evidence of construct validity. If a scale has a high index of internal consistency, we know that the items are substantially intercorrelated. They are working together to measure the same underlying variable. This constitutes evidence that a construct is being measured. It does not constitute a complete validation. Just because we have proven that *a* construct is being measured does not necessarily mean that the *right* construct is being measured. Internal consistency by itself is not a sufficient validation technique. Other evidence is needed to show that the construct being measured is the construct that is supposed to be measured. Remember, though, that by the very nature of the attitude-scale construction process (Likert and Thurstone, at least) some amount of *content* validity is assured. Content validity and internal consistency are often used in combination in attitude-scale validation. This combination of content validity plus internal consistency supplies at least minimally acceptable evidence of construct validity for attitude scales.

Response to Experimental Manipulating.   A scale ostensibly measuring attitude toward cigarette smoking is administered to a group of student nurses. They participate in a workshop decrying the dangers of cigarette smoking, with lots of statistics linking smoking to lung and heart diseases and to cancer. The tar-colored lungs of a heavy smoker are on display in a jar of formaldehyde. After the workshop an alternate form of the attitude scale is administered. A significantly more negative mean score in attitude toward cigarette smoking is discovered. It is concluded that the scale is indeed measuring attitude toward cigarette smoking (i.e., is valid).

Actually, this validation method might be considered a variant of the known-group method. Mean scores of a group known to be high in the construct are compared with mean scores of a group known to be low (same group, different time, in this instance). There is one caution regarding the experimental-manipulation method. This method is workable only if it can be *assumed* that the experimental treatment is effective. In the attitude-toward-smoking study described in the last paragraph, the validity conclusion is correct only if it can be assumed that the smoking workshop really changed attitude toward smoking. (The same paradigm could be used to test the effectiveness of the experimental treatment. Then, though, the attitude scale must be assumed to be valid.)

Opinion of Judges.   A group of judges is identified and asked to decide whether (1) each scale item falls within the domain of the construct and (2) the items, collectively, are comprehensive in measuring this domain. Judging whether each item falls within the domain of the construct is a reasonable task—if the judges have a clear understanding of the attitude construct. Probably the best judges, in the case of attitude measures, are experts in attitude measurement.

Actually this process—determining whether each item is measuring within the domain of the attitudinal construct—is already partially accomplished in the Likert, Thurstone, and semantic differential scale-construction techniques. In Likert scale construction each item must be keyed by the scale constructor as positive or negative toward the attitudinal object. Items that do not fall in the domain of the construct will be impossible to key. Furthermore, in both the Likert scale and the semantic differential, item analysis identifies items that fail to correlate with the total scale score. Essentially, these items are judged not to be in the construct domain. In theory, consensus of judges could substitute for the statistical analysis of items (although the objectivity of the judges would be a matter of concern). In fact, in the Thurstone scale-construction procedure that is exactly what happens. Judges estimate the degree of positiveness/ negativeness of items. Items on which the judges can't agree are discarded. They are determined not to be effective measures of the construct. In general, judgments about whether items fall within the domain of the construct are accomplished more efficiently and more objectively through statistical item analysis than through the use of judges.

The other judgment, whether the items are comprehensive in measuring the construct, has the same problem as the content-validity method of validation—circumscribing the domain of the construct. No judgmental procedure can completely resolve this dilemma.

Probably the best use of judges in scale construction is in an editorial capacity, to identify ambiguous and poorly worded items. This procedure, though, would enhance reliability more directly than validity.

Response Sets

Validation procedures are designed to demonstrate that a measurement device is measuring what it is supposed to measure. We have seen that another aspect of validity is to ensure that the measurement instrument *isn't* measuring what it *isn't* supposed to measure. One of the most pervasive measurement problems in this regard is *response sets*. Response sets are systematic response patterns based on considerations *other than* the content of the items. For instance, on a Likert attitude scale one respondent may have a propensity to avoid the "undecided" response category, whereas another may overuse this response category. In my research involving attitude and value measurement I have encountered respondents who resist (unconsciously) the use of the "strongly disagree" response category. Obviously, such response tendencies, without regard to item content, can have a negative effect on validity.

There are two response sets that are particularly problematic in affective measurement: acquiescence and social desirability.

Acquiescence Response Set. In our culture (and probably in most others) people are socialized to be agreeable and to agree. "Yes" is a more socially acceptable response, on the average, than "no." When people ask us how we are, we say "Fine." When a waitress asks us whether the food is satisfactory, we say "Yes." When a friend asks for a favor, we assent. We often make a positive response even when such a response is not an honest or heartfelt response. This tendency to acquiesce—to agree—carries over to test-taking behavior. Most of us have some amount of acquiescence response set, but some people have more than others. To the extent that differences in test scores are the result of acquiescence response set rather than of opinions regarding the content of test items, validity is reduced. If a high score on an attitude scale simply indicates that a person is a strong acquiescer, the wrong thing is being measured. Interestingly, the acquiescence response set, like other response sets, has no adverse affect on reliability. If some people consistently agree, item after item, and others consistently do not, this response tendency may even enhance the reliability of the test. But what good is high reliability if the wrong thing is being measured?

Fortunately, the effect of acquiescence responding is easy to control, simply by including half positively worded items and half negatively worded items in the scale (as was suggested for Likert scales in Chapter 2). This does not eliminate acquiescence responding or even reduce it. It simply cancels out its effect. For each point gained by acquiescing to a positively worded item a point is lost by acquiescing to a negatively worded item (because negatively worded items are scored in reverse). The resulting score should be primarily a measure of attitude, with little or no influence from acquiescence response set.

Social-Desirability Response Set. Social-desirability response set is the tendency for test takers to make socially desirable responses to test items at the expense of responses based on their true beliefs and preferences. On many affective test items, identifying the most socially desirable response is easy. Some respondents purposely fake their responses to test items in order to give themselves a better image. Even when overt lying does not occur, there is an unconscious inclination toward social-desirability responding. The measurement problem occurs when this tendency is unequal among respondents. If some test takers gain many points through socially desirable responding and others gain few or no points, than a large portion of variance (spread) in scale scores will be response-set variance rather than substantive (i.e., attitudinal) variance. In extreme instances a scale may be measuring social-desirability response set to a greater extent than it is measuring the affective trait that it is supposed to measure. This is a serious validity problem.

Unfortunately, social-desirability response set has no such easy solution as does acquiescence response set. There are, however, several procedures for reducing this threat to validity. The most direct procedure is to establish a good administrative rapport with respondents. If they can be made to feel unthreatened by the measurement process, they will respond openly and honestly. Assurances of anonymity or confidentiality of responses and scale scores will greatly reduce threat. Fortunately for attitude measurers, attitude scores are seldom used in making decisions about individuals. More often they are used for research and program-evaluation purposes. In such instances individual identities are either not necessary at all (as in group comparisons) or necessary only for data analysis (as in matching attitude scores with some other scores for purposes of correlation). Respondents can thus be promised anonymity.

Other means of controlling for social-desirability response set involve statistical correction of scores based upon the independent measurement of this response set, and the use of forced-choice item format. These procedures are seldom used in attitude measurement but are sometimes employed in the measurement of personality traits and values.

8

Other Methods
of Attitude Assessment

In previous chapters I have described the Likert, Thurstone, Guttman, and
semantic differential attitude-scaling techniques. These were selected because of their popularity among attitude researchers and because of their
relatively good psychometric characteristics. These scaling techniques,
however, are not without shortcomings, as we have seen. There are other
legitimate attitude-scaling techniques, as well as a wide variety of nonscale
attitude-assessment methods. In particular research and evaluation situations, these methods are acceptable or even preferable alternatives to the
popular scaling techniques.

OTHER SCALING METHODS

The Bogardus Social Distance Scale is of primarily historical importance.
Remmers Generalized Attitude Scales are a collection of generic attitude
scales that can be used, without alteration, across classes of attitudinal
objects. Relative-Belief Attitude Scaling is an adaptation of Likert scaling
that was developed by the present author.

Bogardus Social Distance Scale

The Social Distance Scale of Emory Bogardus measures attitude toward
ethnic and racial groups (see Figure 8.1). This scale is actually a specific
application of the Guttman scaling technique. Interestingly, the Social
Distance Scale was published in 1925, long before Louis Guttman formalized his summative scaling procedure. In fact, the Social Distance Scale is
one of the earliest formalized attitude scales to have been published. It has
been used, over the years, to study societal changes in attitude toward
various ethnic and racial groups. It typically has split-half reliability in the

FIGURE 8.1
Bogardus social distance scale.

According to my first feeling reactions, I would willingly
admit members of each ethnic or national group to the
following classifications:

	Russian	Black	Jewish
1. To close kinship by marriage.	_____	_____	_____
2. To my club as personal chums.	_____	_____	_____
3. To my street as neighbors.	_____	_____	_____
4. To employment in my occupation, in my country.	_____	_____	_____
5. To citizenship in my country.	_____	_____	_____
6. As visitors only to my country.	_____	_____	_____
7. Would exclude from my country.	_____	_____	_____

Source: Adapted from Bogardus (1928), p. 27.

low .90s. See Bogardus (1959) for a more thorough presentation on the use
and validity of the Social Distance Scale.

Generalized Attitude Scales

Since attitude scales are specific to attitudinal objects, it is often difficult
to find an existing scale appropriate for use in a particular research project.
Typically, the necessary scale is constructed by each researcher. Shortly
after the Thurstone scaling technique was formalized, Hermann Remmers
and his associates at Purdue University set out to construct generalized
attitude scales, each for use with all cases within a class of social objects.
There were developed, for example, scales for the measurement of attitude
toward *any social group, any practice, any occupation,* and *any institution.*
Sample items from the Scale for Measuring Attitude Toward Any Institution are found in Figure 8.2. A description of the development procedure
for these generalized attitude scales is found in Remmers (1934).

In 1960 Remmers published shortened versions of a number of these
scales under the name Purdue Master Attitude Scales. All of Remmers's

FIGURE 8.2
Sample items from one of Remmers's generalized attitude
scales.

A Scale For Measuring Attitude Toward Any Institution

Ida B. Kelley and H. H. Remmers

Place a check (✓) by each statement with which you agree,
with reference to the following institution: _____

_____ 2. Is the most admirable of institutions. (11.1)

_____ 15. Serves society as a whole well. (9.5)

_____ 22. Inspires no definite likes or dislikes. (6.4)

_____ 28. Gives too little service. (4.5)

_____ 38. Is entirely unnecessary. (2.3)

Source: Abridged and adapted from Figure 19, p. 389
from Educational Measurement and Evaluation, Revised
Edition, by H. H. Remmers and N. L. Gage. Copyright 1943,
1955 (company) by H. H. Remmers and N. L. Gage. Reprinted
by permission of Harper & Row, Publishers, Inc.
    Note: Scale values, ranging from 1.00 to 12.00,
appear in parentheses following each item.

revised scales have 17 items. There are two alternate forms of each scale.
They are Thurstone-type scales, so each item has a favorableness value.
Respondents mark only the items with which they agree. Any number of
items may be marked. The average value for all items marked constitutes
each respondent's attitude score. The Remmers scales have reliability
coefficients ranging from .71 to .92.

There are other generalized attitude scales, in addition to those of
Remmers. The Bogardus Social Distance Scale is actually a generalized
attitude scale toward any racial or ethnic group, and the semantic differential could be considered the ultimate form of generalized attitude scaling.

One problem with generalized attitude scales is that scale items aren't
equally relevant to all objects in a given class. For instance, the item "I
would enjoy this practice if it were changed somewhat" appears in the
Attitude Toward Any Practice Scale (Remmers, 1960). This item seems
more applicable to public and ritualized practices (such as standing up to
sing the national anthem or shaking hands with opponents at a sports
event) than it does to such private practices as counting sheep to get to
sleep, taking an aspirin for a headache, or smoking marijuana. If the fit of

the item to the object becomes too awkward, rapport with respondents is likely to become a problem. This same objection was cited with reference to the semantic differential.

Relative-Belief Attitude Scales

In Likert, Thurstone, and Guttman attitude scales, some items compare the attitudinal object, either directly or indirectly, with similar or alternative objects. For example, here are some attitude items that require an explicit comparison with a specific alternative to the attitudinal object under consideration (the attitudinal object is italicized in each item):

Getting a *divorce* is better than staying in an unhappy marriage.
I believe that the *death penalty* is more humane than life imprisonment.
I would rather have my child in an *open classroom* than in a traditional classroom.

In other attitude items comparison of the attitudinal object with alternative objects is less direct or is merely implied:

Divorce is an acceptable alternative in today's American society.
The *death penalty* is the only appropriate punishment for some crimes.
Children learn to be more sociable in *open classrooms*.

Even when no comparison is stated or implied, the attitude-scale respondent inevitably evaluates the attitudinal object within a relative context. In fact, it could be argued that evaluation is *always* ultimately relative. In any case, it is clear that items requiring comparison of the attitudinal object with alternative objects work well in attitude scales. Some attitudinal objects seem, particularly, to require a relative judgment. How, for instance, can one think about the advantages and disadvantages, the strengths and weaknesses, of a *woman president* other than by comparison with men presidents?

A *woman president* would be very responsible.
A *woman president* would be unable to handle the emotional stress of the presidency.
A *woman president* would be more responsive to the needs of the people.

Another type of *relative-belief* item is one that requires the respondent to estimate the position of her own attitude relative to the attitudinal position of other specific groups or individuals: "Compared with members of the League of Women Voters, my attitude toward a *woman president* is . . ."

Mueller (1985) has focused on this strong contextual framework in which attitudes exist by developing attitude scales comprised entirely of relative-belief items. Figure 8.3, designed to measure attitude toward marijuana, illustrates such a scale. Three kinds of explicit comparisons are required of respondents in this scale: (1) comparison of one's own attitudinal position with the attitudinal positions of other "known" groups (items 1–7), (2) judgments of the harmfulness of marijuana relative to the harmfulness of other drugs (items 8–13), and (3) comparison of marijuana use with a variety of (other) social problems (items 14–20). Other categories of comparative questions are, of course, possible.

The scale presented in Figure 8.3 had an alpha reliability coefficient of .87 when administered to graduate students in a social psychology class and to some of their spouses and friends ($N = 43$). The third category of relative-belief items (comparison with other social problems) was the most effective, with item–total score correlations ranging from .80 to .83. Item-total correlations in category 2 (harmfulness of marijuana relative to other drugs) ranged from .59 to .76 (except for item 13, which correlated only .13). Items in the first category correlated from .19 to .71, with a median correlation of .57. Total scores on this scale correlated highly (in the .70s) with a Likert (Figure 2.1), a Thurstone, and a semantic differential scale measuring attitude toward the same attitudinal object.

The relative-belief attitudinal scaling procedure should be considered experimental at this time. It has been subjected to limited psychometric scrutiny to date. In comparison with some other attitude-scaling techniques, relative-belief scales are very direct in establishing the domain of attitude under consideration. Because every item requires an explicit comparison with an alternative attitudinal object or with a "normative" attitudinal position, all respondents have the same context; they are all working with the same operational definition of *attitude*. The disadvantage of such explicitly comparative items is that respondents are all presumed to have knowledge of the alternative attitudinal objects and of the attitudes of the comparison groups. In the last chapter of this book we will examine in greater depth the establishment of the attitudinal domain, as operationalized by the various scaling procedures that we have studied.

MEASURING ATTITUDE WITH A SINGLE ITEM

The major reason for using multiple items in a scale to measure attitude, rather than using a single item, is to achieve high reliability. We learned in

FIGURE 8.3
Mueller relative-belief attitude scale measuring attitude toward marijuana.

How Do You Feel About Marijuana?

For items 1 to 7 use the following response categories:

     A = definitely more positive
     B = slightly more positive
     C = about the same
     D = slightly more negative
     E = definitely more negative

_____ 1. Relative to how I believe college students view marijuana, my own views on marijuana are:

_____ 2. Relative to how I believe persons over 40 view marijuana, my own views on marijuana are:

_____ 3. Relative to how I believe policemen view marijuana, my own views on marijuana are:

_____ 4. Relative to how I believe doctors view marijuana, my own views are:

_____ 5. Relative to how I believe graduate students in education view marijuana, my own views are:

_____ 6. Relative to how I believe graduate students in arts and sciences view marijuana, my own views are:

_____ 7. Relative to how I believe hippies view marijuana, my own views are:

For items 8 to 13 use the following response categories:

     A = much more harmful to a person
     B = slightly more harmful to a person
     C = no more or less harmful to a person
     D = slightly less harmful to a person
     E = much less harmful to a person

_____ 8. Relative to alcohol, marijuana is:

_____ 9. Relative to cigarettes, marijuana is:

_____10. Relative to fumes from airplane glue, marijuana:

_____11. Relative to amphetamines, marijuana is:

_____12. Relative to barbiturates, marijuana is:

_____13. Relative to caffeine, marijuana is:

(continued)

FIGURE 8.3 (continued)

For items 14 to 20 use the following categories:

            A = strongly agree
            B = agree
            C = no opinion or neutral
            D = disagree
            E = strongly disagree

_____14. Marijuana use is a more serious social problem
           than is racial conflict.

_____15. Marijuana use is a more serious social problem
           than is poverty.

_____16. Marijuana use is a more serious social problem
           than is pollution.

_____17. Marijuana use is a more serious social problem
           than is overpopulation.

_____18. Marijuana use is a more serious social problem
           than is unemployment.

_____19. Marijuana use is a more serious social problem
           than is shoplifting.

_____20. Marijuana use is a more serious social problem
           than is delinquency.

Chapters 2 and 4 that Likert and Thurstone scales of about 20 items typically have reliabilities in the .80s. In Chapter 3 we saw that a well-constructed Likert scale can achieve internal consistency in the .90s. We also saw that a decrease from 47 items to 20 items reduced alpha insignificantly. (Of course, we kept 20 of the best items.) Just how far could the number of items be reduced without a drastic reduction in reliability? Is it possible that attitude could be measured adequately with a single self-report item?

The key to this question is the word *adequately*. With a single item it is not possible to achieve reliability in the .90s or even in the .80s or .70s. It may, under certain conditions, be possible for a single item to achieve reliability in the .40s or .50s.

Such an item must come right to the point. It would be classified as a *feeling* item rather than as a *cognitive* or *behavioral-tendency* item. It would require a rating-type response "scale" with more than the usual five

Likert response categories. In order for any measure to achieve even moderately high reliability, there must be substantial score variance among respondents. In scales, this variance is achieved by summing the scores, and thus cumulating the variance, across all items. With a single item all the variance in scores must come from that item. Such an item, measuring attitude toward abortion, might look like this:

What is your attitude toward abortion?

1	2	3	4	5	6	7	8	9
Strongly oppose				Neutral				Strongly favor

Reporting in the *Journal of Applied Psychology,* Taylor and Parker (1964) illustrated that single-item attitude measurement was indeed viable. They measured physicians' attitudes toward treatment of emotionally disturbed patients, using eight items, such as the following (p. 38):

How do you feel about treating emotionally disturbed patients?

Dislike treating						Like treating
1	2	3	4	5	6	7

They correlated the ratings to these "attitude report questions" with scores on eight counterpart Guttman scales. Correlations ranged from .34 to .70, with four of the eight correlations above .55. No reliability data were reported for the attitude report questions, but reliabilities must have been at least moderate for most items in order to be able to achieve these moderately high validity correlations with the Guttman scales.

Is reliability in the .40s and .50s high enough? The answer to this question is very important and is not well understood by some researchers and practitioners. In research situations where group means are being compared, moderate reliability may be acceptable! This is because error in the measurement of individuals will balance out for the group as a whole. The sum of individual measurement errors in one direction (too high) tends to equal the sum of individual measurement errors in the other direction (too low). When the group mean is computed, these errors will cancel each other out. The mean of raw scores within each group should thus be precisely at the mean of (hypothetical) "true" scores. This will be so for all groups. Such balancing out of measurement errors, however, can be counted on only in relatively large groups. With groups smaller than 30, it is desirable to have a reliability greater than .50. With groups of 100 or larger, measures with reliability as low as .40 may be used.

A common example of research in which a single item is used to measure each opinion or attitude, and in which group scores rather than individual scores are studied, is survey research. In survey research a questionnaire consisting of a number of discretely scored opinion items is administered to groups of people, for purposes of description and comparison.

In interpreting the scores of individuals, however, and in comparing individuals with one another, moderate reliability is *not acceptable!* With a reliability of .50, two individuals in a group, scoring at the 50th and 75th percentiles, respectively (which, on a seven-point response scale, such as in the Taylor and Parker items, is likely to be no more than one raw score point apart), have a probability of .37 of scoring in reverse order on a retesting. Such a magnitude of error is intolerable in making decisions about individuals. Even with a reliability of .80 the probability of such an error is .20.

Low or moderate reliability also has a serious negative effect on correlational research. If attitude scores are being correlated with other measures (such as achievement or personality test scores), low or moderate reliability is not acceptable. (There is a statistical method of estimating what the intercorrelation of two variables *would be* if their reliabilities were perfect, however. This estimation procedure is called the *correction for attenuation.*)

One criticism of single-item measurement, even in research on groups, is that responses are particularly subject to faking and to other response sets. Because the single item is so direct in asking about a particular attitude, it is vulnerable to social-desirability response set. Likewise, there is no control for acquiescence response set, since it is impossible to word half the items negatively and reverse them in scoring.

DISGUISED SELF-REPORT TECHNIQUES

The self-report attitude-measurement techniques that have been reviewed to this point are relatively straightforward concerning what is being measured. While respondents may not always use the word *attitude* in labeling the measure, the fact that they are being asked, either directly or indirectly, to *evaluate* a particular object is not disguised. In this section we will look at several disguised self-report techniques—techniques in which respondents are required to respond to stimuli that afford no clue to the fact that *attitude* is the construct being measured. The potential advantage of disguised measurement is obvious. The effect of social-desirability response set is eliminated.

Two major categories of disguised techniques will be discussed: those which appear to the respondent to be cognitive or skill tests, such as knowledge tests, tests of logic, memory tests, and perception tasks (Cook and Selltiz, 1964, label these "objective tasks"), and those which encourage free or open-ended responses to relatively unstructured stimuli (sometimes called projective techniques).

Cognitive Tests

Examples of attitude measures disguised as cognitive tests are the error-choice technique (Hammond, 1948) and a technique involving the use of logical syllogisms (Thistlethwaite, 1950). The error-choice technique requires the construction of two-response, multiple-choice knowledge items about the attitudinal object. However, neither response provided is the correct answer. One response errs in favor of the attitudinal object, the other against it. Sample items from Hammond's Attitude Toward Labor/Management Scale are the following:

1. Average weekly wage of the war worker in 1945 was: (a) $37.00, (b) $57.00. (p. 39)
2. Financial reports show that out of every dollar: (a) 16 cents, (b) 3 cents is [sic] profit. (p. 48)

Since these are very obscure facts, and since neither response is correct, respondents have no choice but to guess. The assumption is that their guesses will be influenced by their attitudinal preferences. The reliabilities of Hammond's scales range from the high .70s to the high .80s. Other attempts to measure attitude through biased errors in knowledge have had somewhat lower reliabilities.

The following item is from Thistlethwaite's logical-syllogism attitude measure. Respondents are to judge the logical correctness of the conclusion.

Given: If production is important, then peaceful industrial relations are desirable.
Given: If production is important, then it is a mistake to have Negroes for foremen and leaders over whites.
Therefore: If peaceful industrial relations are desirable, then it is a mistake to have Negroes for foremen and leaders over whites. (p. 444)

The conclusion in this argument is not logically correct. But a group of anti-Negro, white respondents was found to make significantly more mistakes in logic on a scale of such items than on neutral or nonattitudinal logical syllogisms.

Other examples of "objective" tasks used to measure attitude involve (1) distortions of memory, in which, after being exposed to a factual or persuasive communication, respondents are assumed to be able to recall more facts or arguments that support their own attitudinal position than those which don't (Horowitz and Horowitz, 1938; Doob, 1953), and (2) estimation of group attitudinal position, in which respondents are expected to project their own attitude to the group (Travers, 1941; Wallen, 1943).

Projective Techniques

The rationale for all projective techniques is that when presented with an unstructured or ambiguous stimulus having to do with the attitudinal object, and asked to respond, testees must draw on beliefs and attitudes in their own psyche, since there is no other source of response.

In a sense *all* disguised techniques require respondents to project their attitudes into the realm of cognitive knowledge or judgment. What distinguishes the techniques presented here (projective techniques) from those just presented (cognitive tests) is a lower level of structuring of the respondent's task (free-response items) and a higher level of subjectivity in attitudinal scoring.

Most closely associated with projective personality tests, such as the Thematic Apperception Test (Murray, 1943), are attitude-measurement techniques in which respondents are shown a picture containing an instance of the attitudinal object and are asked to tell a story about the picture. In some applications the picture is somewhat abstract, or it may be shown for only a few seconds. Both of these conditions increase the projective nature of the task. Variants of this technique are for respondents to be required to choose between alternate stories or explanations and for the test administrator to ask leading questions such as "Who was the black man with the broom?" when in fact there was no black man with a broom in the picture.

Sentence-completion and story-completion tasks constitute another type of projective attitude-measurement technique. They may or may not be disguised. For instance, the item "Negro body odor . . ." is not at all disguised. The item "Some people are poor and it's their own fault. What people?" is disguised, but its response may or may not focus on the intended attitudinal object. One way to supply sentence stems or story beginnings containing the attitudinal object and still disguise the purpose of attitude measurement is to intersperse dummy items among the real ones.

Examples of attitude measurement with incomplete sentences are illustrated by Rotter and Willerman (1947) and Zeligs (1937).

Several researchers have used doll play as an index of attitude. Dolls identifiable by race, sex, religious affiliation, and other social and demographic characteristics have been used. Children (and sometimes adults) have been given tasks such as "Select which dolls you would invite to a party" (Pushkin, 1967), "Create a dramatic scene" (Dubin, 1940), role playing (Hartley and Schwartz, 1948), and forming social groups (Kuethe, 1964). As with other projective techniques, attitude scoring of doll-play tasks is very subjective. In addition, the scope of attitudinal objects is limited to characteristics and identifications that can be attributed to the dolls. Doll play is a clinical measurement tool that may be used with young children or with disturbed children and adults when an open-ended technique is required.

An annotated compilation of 11 doll-play and other projective attitude-measurement instruments for use with preschool and primary-level children has been published by Walker (1973, pp. 45–63). Many of these measures have been designed specifically to measure racial attitudes. All have limited (or no) reliability and validity data.

Evaluation of Disguised Techniques

Disguised techniques are not widely used in attitude measurement. They are generally less reliable than the more traditional attitude scales. The highly structured and objectively scored disguised measures (such as error-choice and logical-syllogisms tests) are difficult and time-consuming to construct. The projective techniques are costly to administer and difficult to score. The only serious advantage of disguised techniques is that they are not subject to faking. In the case of attitude measurement, this is not a great advantage. Faking is not as serious a problem in attitude measurement as it is in the measurement of personality traits. People are usually willing to share their opinions regarding most attitudinal objects. This is especially true if responses are anonymous, or if their attitude scores are not used to make decisions about them. One or both of these conditions are normally the case in attitude research.

INTERVIEWING

An interview is, basically, an orally administered questionnaire. It may be used to assess one or more attitudes or a variety of attitudes, beliefs, and opinions on one or several topics. If circumstances required it, a Likert or

Thurstone attitude scale could be administered in an interview format. Usually, though, responses to interview questions are analyzed separately rather than being summed to a scale score.

The greatest benefit of interviewing as a mechanism for data collection is the face-to-face interaction between interviewer and interviewee. People are often more willing to share their opinions orally than in a written format. If the interviewer gains the trust of the interviewee, forthright and extensive responses can be elicited. The interviewer can also clarify ambiguous questions and use his judgment to interject additional, "probing" questions where elaboration or clarification of a response is required. Even gestures, tone of voice, hesitation in responding, and facial expression can provide insight to nuances in attitude and act as cues for further probing.

The interview questionnaire, or "schedule" as it is called, may be highly structured, with very specific questions and multiple-choice response categories. Such a format facilitates data analysis and quantitative comparison across individuals and groups, but fails to take advantage of the major strength of the interview technique—free and forthright flow of opinion in the interviewee's own words and cognitive context. A completely unstructured interview format, on the other hand, may digress from the topic of the interview. Further, verbal responses from unstructured items are difficult to tabulate reliably. Analysis of such responses is highly subjective, and the researcher's biases are more likely to enter into the resultant conclusions. Perhaps the best compromise is to include both structured and unstructured questions in interview schedules. Response categories for structured questions should be based upon the anticipated range of responses (perhaps from a pilot study using open-ended questions). Each structured question may be followed by an open-ended question inviting interviewees' comments or elaboration. Or the order of structured and unstructured questions may be reversed.

Questions of reliability and validity are somewhat awkward to address with interview data, especially unstructured interview questions. Interview data are considered reliable if the same conclusions regarding respondents' attitudes result from two separate interviews of the same subject. There are three possible sources of unreliability: (1) inconsistency in responding on the part of the interviewee, (2) mistakes or inconsistencies in recording by the interviewer, and (3) arbitrariness or bias in interpretation by the researcher who analyzes and summarizes the data.

Several mechanisms are available for controlling these sources of unreliability: (1) Questions should be edited for clarity. (2) Some questions can be repeated, in the same or slightly different wording, at different places in an interview. (3) Taping the interview will ensure accurate recording. (4) Repeating the interview at a later time, with the same or a different interviewer, is a check for both consistency of responses and consistency of recording. (5) Having a second and independent researcher analyze the recorded data and draw conclusions verifies the objectivity and consistency of the interpretation process.

Interviews are often used for research involving the description and comparison of the opinions and attitudes of groups. They are also sometimes used for making decisions regarding the hiring and school admission of individuals and in making clinical assessments. In the hands of a skilled interviewer, interview data can be extremely rich and colorful. This method of data collection is especially useful in uncovering attitudes and opinions regarding a particular social issue that have not been anticipated in advance by the researcher. The open-ended nature of interview responses and the face-to-face interaction, with discretionary power for the interviewer to reword and add questions, constitute the strength of the interview method. However, in situations where the constructs to be measured are well crystallized and the research questions are highly structured, these qualitatively rich data rarely justify the high cost of a one-on-one data-collection procedure. The interviewer and the data interpreter are invested with great responsibility for the quality of interview-based research conclusions. The data are as good or as bad as the skill and objectivity of these researchers.

Because of its subjective nature and because there is typically only one item per attitude or issue, interview data are, even at best, less reliable than data from well-constructed psychological scales. For group comparisons reliability may be adequate. But interview data should be weighted less heavily than other, more reliable data sources in making decisions about individuals.

OBSERVATION

Observation is the basic method of data collection in *all* scientific research. The word *empirical*, as in *empirical research*, is nearly synonymous with the word *observational*. In the physical sciences fairly direct observation can be carried out on many variables of interest: wind speed, body temperature, compression ratio, growth of bacteria in a culture, thickness of a particular rock stratum, movement of a star over time, and the molecular structure of a chemical compound. In the study of mental traits and characteristics only behavior can be observed and measured. The existence and magnitude of psychological constructs must be inferred.

Responses to test items are, of course, behaviors, and these are indeed "observed" by researchers. But responses to test items are contrived behaviors. They may or may not represent a subject's real inclination toward the stimulus object. Another category of human behavior that can be observed as a basis for inferences about psychological constructs is *naturally occurring behavior*. The measurement by observation of naturally occurring behavior is the subject of this section. It should be noted that, unlike all the measurement techniques that have been reviewed to this point, observation of naturally occurring behavior is *not* a self-report technique.

Observation requires an observer and an observational plan. In the measurement of attitude, those behaviors that are presumed to relate to the attitude in question must be recorded or tallied. Measurements of this type are subject to the same criteria of quality as are all measurement techniques: reliability and validity. High-quality observational measurement requires an expert and objective observer, careful selection of behavior situations and of specific behaviors to be observed, a systematic procedure for recording behaviors, and an objective interpretation of the recorded behaviors in making inferences about attitude.

Usually an observer records the behaviors of a single subject. Under certain conditions two or more subjects may be studied by a single observer. The observation plan must specify the behavior setting in which the observation is to occur (e.g., classroom, playground, office, home) and the frequency and length of observation sessions (e.g., 15 minutes twice each day for two weeks). For attitude measurement these decisions are particularly crucial, since only behaviors relevant to the object of attitudinal measurement are of interest.

It is preferable to record behaviors *during* the observation period. If this is not possible, recording should be done soon after observation, in order to maintain objectivity and avoid errors of memory. The observer is frequently in the presence of the subject. Sometimes, however, the observer is concealed (as behind a one-way mirror). The obtrusive presence of the observer raises questions about the observational process's affect on the behaviors being recorded. Observers must be objective and accurate in recording behaviors. The training of observers is standard procedure in observational research. The reliability of observations can be tested by comparing the data of two (or more) independent observers over the same behavior samples.

The recording of behavior may vary substantially in amount of detail and in structuredness. One of the most informal and least structured observational assessment procedures is *anecdotal records*. Here the observer simply writes down, in anecdotal form, behaviors thought to be relevant to the social or psychological construct under study (e.g., attitude toward science, motivation, disruptive behavior, or social adjustment). This kind of observational data is frequently found in letters of recommendation and in teachers' reports to parents. Anecdotal-record data may be collected in a single session, or a simple observational schedule may be followed. A structured behavior-recording form is not often used. This leaves the selection of relevant behavior to the discretion of the observer. It is a good practice to record the behavior of interest immediately following its occurrence. And description of the behavior should be recorded separately from its interpretation.

In order to increase the objectivity and the reliability of observation, a structured observation form is frequently used. Such a form involves preselection and operationalization of the target behaviors, thereby freeing the observer from these judgmental responsibilities. A common procedure is to develop a checklist of behaviors to be recorded and to have observers tally these behaviors at fixed intervals (e.g., every 15 seconds, or each meaningful behavior unit). An example of a recording scheme commonly used in studying the classroom verbal interaction of teacher and students is Flanders's Interaction Analysis System (Flanders, 1970). Teacher behavior categories include such entries as "Praises [students]," "Asks questions," "Accepts ideas of students," and "Criticizes students." (This instrument aggregates student behavior and thus cannot produce attitudinal or other psychological scores for individual students.) For a thorough discussion of the construction and use of observation checklists in attitude measurement, see Henerson, Morris, and Fitz-Gibbon (1978, pp. 108–23).

An alternative to having a trained observer physically present in the behavior setting, tallying behavior as it occurs, is to record the behavior electronically for later analysis, using an audio or video tape recorder. This allows greater flexibility in the scheduling of observers. It also allows repeated analysis of a single behavior sample for purposes of training observers, verifying reliability, and developing or revising the recording form or checklist.

The final step in the process of attitude measurement via observation is to convert the tallied behavior record into attitude scores (or whatever psychological construct is being studied). If a highly structured recording form has been used, the scoring of psychological constructs is relatively straightforward, since the recording system has been devised specifically to record behavior relevant to the construct in question. If a more informal recording procedure (such as anecdotal records) has been used, considerable interpretation is called for at this stage. Just as the tallies of two or more observers can be compared to test for reliability in the use of a highly structured recording system, so the scores of two or more interpreters can be compared to test for objectivity in the interpretation process.

The reliability of observational measures is generally somewhat lower than that of well-constructed scales. An advantage of observation is that the problems of faking and social-desirability response set are eliminated, although response sets on the part of observers (such as leniency and halo effect) are introduced. Probably the single biggest drawback of observational measurement is cost. Large amounts of observational time are required to obtain relatively small amounts of psychological data, because behaviors relative to a particular attitudinal object may be infrequent among naturally occurring behaviors. One-on-one "administration" is another high-cost factor of observational measurement. In addition, observers and their equipment must be transported to the site of the naturally occurring behavior, and observers must be trained. Still another consideration is the necessity of obtaining the permission of observees. Some people do not like to be observed. Nonetheless, this form of measurement goes a long way toward assuring that the behaviors measured are not contrived but represent subjects' normal, day-to-day inclinations toward an attitudinal object. The measurement of psychological constructs by observation is *necessary* for small children and for both children and adults who, because of language, physical, or emotional disability, cannot respond to a self-report instrument.

PHYSIOLOGICAL TECHNIQUES

Physiological techniques of attitude measurement are indices based on bodily states that are controlled by the autonomic nervous system. Included in this category are all circulatory, respiratory, and digestive functions, as well as glandular and sensory processes. Among possible measures of these autonomically controlled bodily processes are the following: heart rate, blood pressure, body chemistry, body temperature, water balance, rate of breathing, salivation, and basal metabolism.

Physiological measures are attractive to psychological researchers because they are almost entirely beyond volitional control, thus precluding falsification of responses even more surely than do disguised measures. In addition, interval-level measurement, a relatively sophisticated level of measurement, can be achieved with physiological measures. The difference, for instance, between a finger temperature of 98.2° and 98.7° is an interval-level measurement. Furthermore, measuring physiological phenomena directly seems, somehow, to get closer to the roots of psychological states and traits.

In 1884 and 1885, respectively, William James and Charles Lange, working independently in different parts of the world, proffered the theory that bodily changes are directly related to emotional states (James and

Lange, 1922). Since that time it has become clear, through efforts on the part of hundreds—perhaps thousands—of psychological researchers trying to prove the theory, that the relationship of physiological states to emotional states is very complex. There is not a simple one-to-one relationship. Physiological activation is certainly a necessary condition for emotion, but differentiation among emotional states is brought about through the cognitive orientation of subjects. This principle was illustrated quite graphically by Schachter and Singer (1962). These researchers injected subjects with either adrenalin or ephedrin in order to produce stimulation of the sympathetic nervous system similar to that found in strong emotion. In this condition of activation subjects could readily be manipulated into states of euphoria, anger, or amusement simply by varying their cognitive setting.

Galvanic Skin Response

Two physiological measurement techniques have been studied extensively in their relation to attitude: galvanic skin response (GSR), which is a measure of skin conductance of electrical current, and pupillary dilation. GSR readings are obtained by "gluing" electrodes to the skin and passing a weak electrical current between them. Changes in the electrical conductance of the skin occur with the introduction of various psychological stimuli to the subject.

Many studies relating GSR to attitude have dealt with racial prejudice: A number of these studies have shown significantly different skin conductance levels between racially prejudiced and nonprejudiced white subjects in response to the presence of, the mention of, or pictures of blacks. In one of the most successful of these studies, Cooper and Pollock (1959) found a rank-order correlation of .82 between average GSR responses and average scores on a paired-comparisons test, for 53 subjects, in response to the names of nine ethnic and national groups.

Despite some success in measuring attitudes, GSR is seldom the method of preference in attitude studies. One reason is the cost. Equipment is cumbersome and expensive, skilled technicians are necessary for administration, and individual administration is required. Furthermore, GSR reliability can be quite low due to sensitivity to physiological, psychological, and situational interference. GSR readings may be affected by sudden sounds, incidental thoughts, body temperature, skin thickness, speech, body movement, feelings of expectations or relief, placement and size of electrode, threshold level, different conductance levels across respondents, and changing conduction levels, over time, for a single subject. And finally, since GSR is basically an index of sympathetic activation, it is not sensitive to direction of attitude: strong *positive* attitudes and strong *negative* attitudes may produce similar GSR readings.

Pupillary Dilation

Gump (1962) reports that for centuries Chinese jade dealers have used pupillary dilation as an index of customers' evaluations of particular stones. Early in the twentieth century German scientists noted a correlation between central nervous system activity and pupil size (Bumke, 1911). In 1929 Kuntz reported that emotions of both pleasure and fear are often accompanied by pupillary dilation.

More recently a series of publications by Eckhard Hess, from 1960 through 1966, caused a flurry of excitement. Hess reported that positive attitude was associated with pupillary dilation and negative attitude with constriction: "There is a continuum of responses that ranges from extreme dilation for . . . pleasing stimuli to extreme constriction for distasteful [stimuli]" (Hess, 1965, p. 6). He found, for instance, that dilation occurred when heterosexual male and female subjects viewed pictures of nude and seminude members of the opposite sex and that constriction occurred when subjects were shown pictures of crippled children and of dead soldiers. Not all of Hess's findings, however, were consistent with these—especially those regarding negative stimuli. Sometimes negative stimuli, too, caused dilation.

John Woodmansee attempted to replicate Hess's findings and to further pursue the pupillary response for attitudinal relationships. He lists a series of intervening variables not controlled by Hess. Woodmansee was unable to replicate the pupillary constriction response to negative stimuli reported by Hess. In fact, Woodmansee concludes that pupil size does not measure attitude in any direct way at all but rather is an index of "arousal, attentiveness, interest, and perceptual orienting" (Woodmansee, 1970, p. 532). This conclusion places pupillary dilation in the category with GSR, as an index of physiological activation but not of any particular emotion, attitude, or psychological state.

For a detailed discussion and an assessment of physiological techniques in attitude measurement see Mueller (1970).

SUMMARY

In this chapter we have reviewed a large variety of procedures for the measurement of attitude. Altogether in this book we have seen nearly every formalized measurement technique available. It should be clear by now that none of these techniques or procedures is the best one to use in all attitude-measurement situations. Rather, the strengths and weaknesses of each technique must be weighed against the requirements of each attitude-measurement occasion.

If high reliability is of paramount importance and the attitudinal issue or object is clearly defined, a highly structured multi-item scale, such as the Likert or Thurstone scales, will be the most efficient measurement technique. Even then, reliability is marginal for use in comparing individuals, and questions of validity (especially socially desirable responding) must be raised. In a group-comparison research situation a single self-report item or a very short scale may be most efficient and can be administered in a questionnaire or interview mode.

Disguised techniques that are structured (e.g., error-choice or logical-syllogisms tests) are fairly reliable and, of course, are not subject to faking or social-desirability response set. They are difficult to construct. Projective techniques are very subjective to score and therefore tend to have low reliability. In the hands of a skilled clinical psychologist, this problem is at least partially overcome.

Generalized scales, including the semantic differential, are quite reliable, but not all items may be equally applicable to all attitudinal objects. Due to the general nature of all items, this operationalization of the attitude construct tends to be very directly affective (rather than cognitive or conative). The susceptibility of generalized scales to faking is about the same as for other relatively direct (nondisguised) self-report methods.

Interviewing, observation, and physiological techniques are substantially more costly than are group-administered paper-and-pencil instruments. Observation is necessary with very young, severely disabled (physically or emotionally), and uncooperative "respondents." A significant limitation of observation in attitude measurement is that behavior toward some attitudinal objects occurs infrequently. Interviewing is particularly valuable when the confidence of respondents must be gained in order to ensure honest responses (or any responses at all). Interviewing is also useful in program-evaluation and exploratory-research situations, where research questions have not been tightly conceptualized and the range of possible opinions regarding a social or attitudinal issue is not fully known. Both interviewing and observation are subject to the subjective judgments of the measurement researchers. Reliability, thus, can vary substantially. Physiological techniques seem to have no bright future in the measurement of attitude at this time.

Several researchers who, over the years, have used and studied attitude-measurement techniques have suggested a *multiple-indicator* approach to attitude measurement. Because every known technique has one or more serious weaknesses and because even the best techniques have less than perfect reliability, it is reasoned that using more than one technique to measure an attitude will, in part, compensate for the weaknesses of each technique. Each measure can be used to verify the measurement of the other measures—a kind of "convergent" validity. Proponents of such an approach are Campbell (1950), Cook and Selltiz (1964), and Summers (1970). While the value of such an approach is indisputable, it is carried out infrequently in practice. This is in part because of the increased measurement cost and in part because attitude researchers and practitioners seem to trust the measurement data from their single technique, whatever the technique. I think the multiple-indicator approach is a fine idea. It seems not to be highly realistic, though. The next best solution may be for individual attitude researchers to be cognizant of the weaknesses of their chosen techniques, to try to overcome these weaknesses where possible, and to report them as limitations of their conclusions.

9
Conclusions

Attitude has been an extremely popular and important focus in social research and evaluation during the last half century. As a consequence, a large number and a great diversity of attitude-measurement techniques have been developed, many of which are described and critiqued in this book. In this chapter we will take stock, both of the attitude-measurement enterprise and of the attitude construct itself. This summary will have three major parts: (1) the state of the art of attitude measurement (the psychometric quality of attitude-measurement instruments), (2) the inter-relationship of beliefs, attitudes, and values (the "best" conceptual model for the attitude construct), and (3) the dimensionality of the attitude construct (is attitude uni- or multidimensional?) A brief concluding section references sources for existing attitude scales.

STATE OF THE ART OF ATTITUDE MEASUREMENT

Judged within the context of psychological measurement, and particularly within the domain of affect, the art of attitude measurement is in relatively respectable condition. There is a large variety of attitude-measurement techniques and procedures from which to choose, each with its unique advantages and disadvantages. Most of these techniques can achieve moderately high reliability; some can achieve very high reliability.

The most serious weakness in attitude measurement is in the realm of validity. Specifically, with many attitude-measurement techniques, responses can be faked. This is a universal problem in affective measurement. It is less serious in the case of attitude, though, than with many other affective constructs. For most attitudinal objects, people are perfectly willing to express their opinions frankly and honestly. The caveat is that attitude scores may not be used to evaluate individual respondents or for any decision making that involves sanctions.

The other important validity question is, of course, the prediction of

97

behavior from attitude scores. A thorough discussion of this issue appeared in Chapter 7 and will not be repeated here. Suffice it to say that attitude toward an object does *not* consistently coincide with each and every behavioral instance toward that object. Nor is it reasonable to expect such an occurrence. People typically have "mixed" attitudes toward objects rather than "pure" (extreme and dogmatic) positive or negative attitudes. It seems obvious, then, that they will have "mixed" (positive and negative) behaviors toward these same objects. Furthermore, it is clear that behaving within a particular situation involves contingencies that confound behavioral preferences and intentions. It is probably correct to conclude that, "all else being equal," people would routinely behave according to their attitudinal predispositions. But life situations are complex, all else is rarely equal, and we must continuously compromise among our contingencies—attitude being but one of these.

INTERRELATIONSHIP OF BELIEFS, ATTITUDES, AND VALUES

In Chapter 1 the relationships of both beliefs and values to attitudes were discussed. It was concluded that positive *attitude* toward an object results from *beliefs* that the object is positively associated with the fulfillment of important *values* and/or from beliefs that the object is negatively associated with (or dissociated from) disvalued objects and concepts. Negative attitude, conversely, results from beliefs that the attitudinal object is dissociated from highly revered values and/or positively associated with disvalued objects and concepts.

Fishbein (1963, 1967a) has formalized this interrelationship mathematically (1963, p. 233):

$$A_o = \Sigma\, Ba$$

where: A_o = *attitude* toward an object
Σ = the sum (for all beliefs about the object)
B = *strength of belief* that the object is associated with another object or concept
a = *evaluative aspect* of B (value of the object or concept with which the attitudinal object is believed to be associated)

Fishbein, interestingly, avoids formal use of the term *value*, instead talking about the "evaluative aspect" of the belief, or evaluation of the object or concept with which the attitudinal object is believed to be associated—which he calls the "related object" or "related concept." (Although, in preliminary discussion of his model, Fishbein describes attitudinal statements as belief statements "associating the object of belief with some other object, concept, *value* [emphasis mine], or goal" [Fishbein, 1967b, p. 259].)

An example will serve to illustrate this model. In a scale measuring attitude toward instructional use of computers, we might find the following item: "Computers enhance academic achievement." In this item, "computers" is the attitudinal object, and "enhance" establishes an association of this object with the value (or value-related other concept) "academic achievement." A positive association with a positively valued *other concept* constitutes a positive *evaluative aspect*. Agreement or disagreement with this belief statement (and the extent of such agreement) constitutes the *strength of belief*. Both evaluative aspect and strength of belief can vary, both in direction and in magnitude. Their product, across all relevant belief statements, is attitude.

Rosenberg (1956), in a very similar but less formalized attitude model, is very direct in his use of the value construct. According to Rosenberg, attitude is a function of (1) "the rated importance of each *value* [emphasis mine] associated with the object" and (2) "the rated potency of the object for achieving or blocking the realization of that value" (p. 367). The latter he labels "perceived instrumentality" (p. 368). Thus Fishbein's *evaluative aspect* is, essentially, Rosenberg's *value importance*, and Fishbein's *strength of belief* is Rosenberg's *perceived instrumentality*. The models are almost identical, one major difference being that Rosenberg believes that all of a person's value-imbued beliefs about an object are *summed* in effecting an attitudinal position, whereas Fishbein maintains that they are *averaged*.

Fishbein has done considerable research in testing his theory and in examining it against existing attitude-scaling methods. One of his conclusions is that differences among respondents in Thurstone scale scores are primarily determined by the *evaluative aspect* component, whereas differences in Likert scale scores are primarily determined by the *strength of belief* component (Fishbein, 1967b). The analysis for these conclusions is illustrated in Figure 9.1.

DIMENSIONALITY OF THE ATTITUDE CONSTRUCT

One remaining issue, which has been addressed from several perspectives throughout the preceding chapters but which has never been brought to closure, is the question of how broadly or narrowly the attitude construct should be conceptualized. Stated differently, is attitude a unidimensional or a multidimensional construct? There are actually two aspects of the dimen-

FIGURE 9.1
Analysis of Likert and Thurstone scale items by Fishbein's attitude model.

	Evaluative Aspect (Value Importance)*	Strength of Belief (Perceived Instrumentality)*
Likert Scales	Items are keyed as either positive or negative. No finer value distinction is made.	Five levels of agreement are possible, from "strongly agree" to "strongly disagree." Most variance in Likert scale scores is from this source.
Thurstone Scales	Items are finely calibrated in favorableness toward the attitudinal object, through judges' ratings. Most Thurstone scale variance derives from this source.	Respondents either agree or disagree with each item. No finer strength-of-belief distinction is made.

Note: Asterisked labels are from Rosenberg's model.

sionality question, which may be examined separately: (1) Can a person hold more than one attitude toward a single attitudinal object? and (2) Does attitude have the same denotation when applied to different objects?

All of the attitude scales that have been studied result in a single score, which seems to imply a unidimensional conceptualization. What is more, in all attitude-scaling techniques, some effort has been made to achieve internal consistency. In some techniques, most notably Guttman scaling, extreme emphasis is placed specifically upon unidimensionality. At the same time, in an effort to achieve content and construct validity, constructors of Likert and Thurstone scales are urged to collect a broad array of opinion statements representing the entire universe of opinions about the attitudinal object. As a result, respondents to such scales can achieve the same score through agreement with different combinations of beliefs and feelings toward the attitudinal object. Gordon Allport recognized this dilemma in 1935 when he noted that two individuals may have the same degree of affect toward an object yet differ "qualitatively" in their attitude toward it. For example, two people may both have a moderately positive attitude toward the church, but one may be attracted to the church primarily for its spiritual qualities (association with God, heaven, morality, and so forth), whereas the other may like the church primarily as an instrument for the fulfillment of social needs.

This line of reasoning leads us to examine the complexity of attitudinal objects. Simple attitudinal objects such as toothbrushes, watermelons, and parking lots don't seem to raise suggestions of multidimensionality. These are relatively simple, single-function objects. To the extent that they fulfill that function well, they are liked; to the extent that they don't, they are disliked. More complex objects, though, engender more diverse opinions and thus more complex attitudes. I may like an automobile for its power, luxury, handling, and status but dislike its lack of economy, size, and country of origin. Or I may feel that a particular automobile is fine for delivering pizza but not for delivering dignitaries.

In part, the problem of multidimensionality of attitude toward complex objects can be resolved by dividing the object into smaller and less complex elements on the basis of component parts, specific functions, or particular contexts. I may, for instance, have a positive attitude toward a particular automobile *as a pizza-delivery vehicle,* but a negative attitude toward the same automobile *as a limousine.* Or I may like the *economic policies* of the president but not his *moral policies.*

Exactly when to subdivide complex objects into components for purposes of measurement is not an easy decision. In general, psychological research is facilitated by the use of tightly defined, unidimensional constructs. Scores on unidimensional scales have a clear and precise psychological meaning. But in real life people must often deal with objects, no matter how complex, as integral entities. If I don't have the luxury to allow both the purchase of a pizza-delivery vehicle and a limousine, I must develop an *overall* attitudinal position toward *every* prospective vehicle and purchase the one that best fulfills my combined needs. Likewise, I must decide either to vote for the president in the next election or to vote against him. In order to make this decision, my separate attitudinal positions toward components of "the president" must be combined to effect a single, composite attitudinal position. In fact, our attitudes toward *persons* constitutes one of the clearest examples of the formation of global or summary attitudes toward highly complex attitudinal objects. As Newcomb concludes, after a thorough and insightful discussion of the attitude-dimensionality issue, "it is likely that we form meaningful *generalized* attitudes about any object, however complex" (Newcomb, Turner, and Converse, 1965, p. 53).

Further evidence for the existence of meaningful generalized attitudes is the fact that separate attitude scales toward the same attitudinal object, constructed either by the same or by different scaling methods, tend to intercorrelate highly—sometimes nearly as highly as their respective reliabilities will permit. It has also been my observation, in the construction of Likert attitude scales, that the highest-correlating items with total scale score are frequently direct feeling items (e.g., "I do not like open classrooms"), rather than highly specific belief items (e.g., "Open classrooms result in higher levels of student achievement") or behavioral-tendency items (e.g., "I would prefer sending my child to a school with open classrooms").

The other aspect of the attitude-dimensionality issue is the likelihood that attitudes toward substantially *different* objects are themselves substantially different in semantic meaning. A positive attitude toward Golden Delicious apples, for instance, is likely to reflect a taste and/or nutritional attraction. A positive attitude toward one's boss, in contrast, may connote respect and/or friendship. Likewise, a positive attitude toward one's boss is likely to be qualitatively different from a positive attitude toward one's spouse or one's lover. And these, in turn, connote different qualities of affect or evaluation than do attitudes toward one's dog, heat pumps, spelunking, smoking cigarettes, or capital punishment. Plato made a similar observation when he distinguished between eros (erotic or sexual love) and agape (spiritual or brotherly love).

It certainly begins to seem as though attitude is not attitude is not attitude. From a theoretical perspective this discovery is somewhat disconcerting. How can social scientists meaningfully use a construct that has a different meaning from one application instance to another? From a practical perspective, however, there is no serious problem. It is not normally the case that one's attitude toward one object is compared with one's attitude toward a substantially different object ("Do you have a more positive attitude toward Golden Delicious apples or toward Martin Luther King?"). In comparing attitudes toward similar objects the same dimension or dimensions of attitude meaning are used.

One last question in determining the meaning of *attitude* in a particular measurement situation is, Who determines the *attitude* definition, the scale constructor or the scale respondent? The extreme case of the *attitude* definition being established by the scale constructor is Guttman scaling, where the items specify a very narrow and specific context of meaning. Similarly, the relative-belief scales described in Chapter 8 establish a narrowly focused context for the meaning of *attitude*. Far to the other extreme are the semantic differential, which comes just short of simply asking respondents directly what their attitude toward the attitudinal object is, and the single-item attitude-measurement technique, which does exactly that. With these techniques there is no guarantee that each respondent uses the same definition of *attitude*. The fact that semantic differential scales routinely achieve very high internal consistency and that these scales correlate highly with other kinds of scales toward the same attitudinal object is further support for Newcomb's notion of generalized affect.

SOURCES OF ATTITUDE SCALES

Literally tens of thousands of attitude scales have been constructed and used throughout the history of social science research. Many of these scales are no longer available at all. Some are available only informally, through direct contact with each scale constructor. But several hundred such scales are available in volumes developed specifically for this purpose. These compendia supply references to existing scales, and in some cases descriptive and evaluative psychometric data, and in yet other instances actual copies of the scales. Appendix A is an annotated bibliography of such compendia of attitude-measurement scales.

The single volume that best achieves the goal of a comprehensive compendium of attitude scales, including copies of the scales and psychometric data about each, is *Scales for the Measurement of Attitudes* (Shaw and Wright, 1967). Other volumes listed in Appendix A review smaller numbers of scales, are specialized within particular application areas (such as mental health attitudes), include references and descriptions but not the scales themselves, and/or do not distinguish clearly between attitude scales and scales measuring other psychological constructs.

APPENDIXES
REFERENCES
INDEX
ABOUT THE AUTHOR

Annotated Bibliography
of Attitude-Measurement
Compendia

Beatty, W. H. (Ed.). (1969). *Improving educational assessment and an inventory of measures of affective behavior.* Washington, DC: Association for Supervision and Curriculum Development, National Education Association.

    The second half of this book is an annotated list of 133 measures of affective behavior by D. J. Dowd and S. C. West. Nearly half are education-specific. The instruments are organized into eight categories: attitudes, creativity, interaction, motivation, personality, readiness, self-concept, and miscellaneous.

    The review for each instrument includes author, availability, description, and variable(s) measured. Reliability and validity data are reported for about half of the measures. Sample items are supplied for some instruments.

Bonjean, C. M., Hill, R. J., & McLemore, S. D. (1967). *Sociological measurement: An inventory of scales and indices.* San Francisco: Chandler.

    This book is an extensive bibliography that references published studies through 1965 using over 2,000 sociological scales and indices. The inventory is organized into 78 categories. All issues of four major sociological journals (*American Journal of Sociology, American Sociological Review, Social Forces,* and *Sociometry*) published between 1954 and 1965 were reviewed for relevant scales. Most are not discussed beyond a basic reference. Forty-seven measures that were cited at least six times in the literature are the subjects of one- to two-page descriptions. Some of these descriptions include psychometric data including coefficients of reproducibility or coefficients of reliability. For most of the scales no validity data are available.

Chun, K. T., Cobb, S., & French, J. R. P., Jr. (1975). *Measures for psychological assessment: A guide to 3,000 original sources and their applications.* Ann Arbor: Institute for Social Research, University of Michigan.

    This book describes 3,000 psychological scales identified in a systematic search of 26 psychological and sociological journals from 1960 to 1970. Most of the scales are value and personality scales rather than attitude scales. The primary substantive focus is mental-health-related measures, but since mental health encompasses a broad variety of personal and social attitudes, traits, and mental conditions, the coverage is quite broad.

The scales themselves are not reproduced. Nor is there technical or critical description. Scales are listed by author and are indexed (and cross-referenced) by several keywords relevant to the scale content. In addition to the original source of each scale, all studies from within the review period in which the scale was subsequently used are cited.

Comrey, A. L., Backer, T. E., & Glaser, E. M. (1973). *A sourcebook for mental health measures*. Los Angeles: Human Interaction Research Institute.

This is a volume of over 1,100 unpublished instruments, inventories, tests, and other measures relating to mental health. The instruments are grouped into 45 categories (e.g., educational adjustment/primary and elementary schools, racial attitudes, student attitudes, teacher attitudes, teacher evaluation). For each instrument there is a brief description that includes such information as purpose, number and type of items, technical data, and availability.

Epstein, I. (1981). *Measuring attitudes toward reading*. New York: LaGuardia Community College, City University of New York.

Fourteen reading-attitude measures are presented with accompanying instructions for administration and scoring, references, and/or sources for additional information. No technical data are presented. All of the instruments, with the exception of one projective measure, are self-report measures.

Ferneau, E. W., Jr. (1973). *Drug abuse research instrument inventory*. Cambridge, MA: Social Systems Analysts.

This volume is intended as an aid in locating measures of constructs relevant for drug abuse studies. The instruments are divided into six categories: attitudes, effects of drugs, characteristics of abusers, access and extent, knowledge about drugs, and drug program evaluation. The inventory is simply a listing of instruments, with no descriptive or psychometric information.

Indik, B. P., Hockmeyer, M., & Castore, C. (1968). *A compendium of measures of individuals, groups, and organizations relevant to the study of organizational behavior* (Tech. Rep. No. 16, Nonr-404). New Brunswick, NJ: Rutgers, The State University.

This file of several hundred measures can be accessed by writing Dr. Bernard P. Indik, Graduate School of Social Work, Rutgers University, New Brunswick, NJ 08903. The measures are reviewed in *People, Groups and Organizations* edited by B. P. Indik and F. K. Berrien, 1968, New York: Teachers College Press. Each instrument in the compendium is described very briefly. Reliability and validity data are largely unavailable. Where available, sample and organizational setting are described.

Johnson, O. G. (1976). *Tests and measurements in child development: Handbook II*. San Francisco: Jossey-Bass.

This is a companion volume to the original handbook (see Johnson & Bommarito, 1971) and includes descriptions of almost 900 additional measures appropriate for use with children up to 18 years of age.

Johnson, O. G., & Bommarito, J. W. (1971). *Tests and measurements in child development: A handbook*. San Francisco: Jossey-Bass.

This book consists of a collection of 316 instruments for assessing cognitive, affective, and sensory-motor attributes. Among the attitude scales included are attitude toward adults, peers, and school. Criteria for including a measure were that it be suitable for use with children between birth and twelve years, available, not commercially published, enough information for effective use, sufficient length to permit development of norms and technical data, and not requiring heavy laboratory equipment.

Included for each instrument are title, author(s), age for which appropriate, constructs measured, type of measure (e.g., projective test, situational interview, etc.), availability, description, administration, scoring, length, sample items, comments from the author or other users, reliability and validity, and usually a brief sample of references supplied by the author.

Kegan, D. L. (1970). *Scales/RIQS: An inventory of research instruments.* Evanston, IL: Northwestern University, Technological Institute.

This inventory contains 360 instruments measuring psychological constructs relevant to organizational theory. Some are attitude scales. Each entry is computer-stored and retrievable. For each instrument the following information is available: author, reference, date, where used (research site and subjects), reliability and validity, construct measured, and comments by the author or person depositing the item in Scales/RIQS. Retrieval from the file can be executed by keying in author, name of instrument, variable, or any desired keyword.

Knapp, J. (1972). *An omnibus of measures related to school based attitudes.* Princeton, NJ: Educational Testing Service, Center for Statewide Educational Assessment.

This book provides summaries of 16 self-report inventories that measure school-based attitudes. Some of the instruments are appropriate for primary and elementary school children, others are for high school students. For each instrument there is a description of contents, subjects, response mode, and scoring procedures. There are also brief evaluative comments for each instrument.

Robinson, J. P., Athanasiou, R., & Head, K. B. (1969). *Measures of occupational attitudes and occupational characteristics.* Ann Arbor: Institute for Social Research, University of Michigan.

This volume and the two following volumes (Robinson et al., 1968, and Robinson et al., 1973) were compiled at the Survey Research Center in the Institute for Social Research at the University of Michigan. The focus is more sociological than psychological; thus attitude scales are in the minority. Many of the scales included measure values and personality traits. Each scale is reproduced in its entirety, together with instructions for administration and scoring. No scale was included without at least minimal evidence of reliability, validity, and standardization data. These data are cited and evaluated.

This volume contains 77 scales measuring job satisfaction, socioeconomic status, occupational interests and values, leadership style, and attitudes toward job and job-related objects (e.g., supervisor, automation, union, management, older workers, mentally ill workers).

Robinson, J. P., Rusk, J. G., & Head, K. B. (1968). *Measures of political attitudes.* Ann Arbor: Institute for Social Research, University of Michigan.

See Robinson et al., 1969 (above).

This volume contains 95 measures of political attitudes, values, orientations (philosophies), and behaviors. The attitude scales include attitude toward government, war, Negroes, Russia, arms control, socialized medicine, big business, civil liberties, and communist and democratic principles.

Robinson, J. P., & Shaver, P. R. (1973). *Measures of social-psychological attitudes.* Ann Arbor: Institute for Social Research, University of Michigan.

    See Robinson et al., 1969 (above).

    This volume reviews 106 psychological and social measures. Most are value and personality scales, measuring such constructs as self-concept, locus of control, anomie, dogmatism, religious orientation, trust in people, and social desirability. One section reviews value inventories containing multiple scales. There are a few attitude scales measuring attitude toward the church, the Bible, and religion.

Rosen, P. (Ed.). (1973). *Attitudes toward school and school adjustment, grades 4–6.* Princeton, NJ: Educational Testing Service.

    This is an annotated bibliography of 31 measures of attitude toward school and school adjustment. Both observational and self-report instruments are included.

Shaw, M. E., & Wright, J. W. (1967). *Scales for the measurement of attitudes.* New York: McGraw-Hill.

    This is a compendium of 176 psychological scales. Most qualify as attitude scales using the narrow definition of *attitude* adopted in the present book. Categories of attitudinal objects include social practices (e.g., discipline of children, sex education, teaching, competition, divorce), social issues (e.g., birth control, academic freedom, socialized medicine, capital punishment, school integration), international issues (e.g., nationalism, world-mindedness, patriotism, communism, militarism, war), abstract concepts (e.g., education, physical fitness, the law, evolution, God), ethnic and national groups (e.g., blacks, Jews, whites, Germans, Chinese, the Soviet Union), significant others (e.g., family, parents, a particular child, self, police, women, old people, the mentally retarded, the blind, the disabled), and social institutions (e.g., college fraternities, mental hospitals, counseling, labor, management, newspapers, church, high school).

    Each scale review includes a copy of the scale, instructions for administration and scoring, a general description, the sample on which it was developed, reliability and validity data, evaluative comments, and the source.

    The scales presented were published between 1930 and 1965. Only scales with some reliability and validity data were included. We are not told what subset of social science literature has been searched in identifying these scales.

Appendix B
Computer Programs for Attitude Scaling

SPSS

Statistical Package for the Social Sciences (SPSS) is a comprehensive and integrated system of packaged statistical programs for data description and hypothesis testing in social science research. It was developed by scientists and statisticians at the National Opinion Research Center at the University of Chicago. SPSSX is the current update and revision (SPSS, Inc., 1983). In addition to procedures for implementing statistical analysis, the SPSS manual has excellent conceptual explanations of these statistics.

SPSS RELIABILITY

Subprogram RELIABILITY computes item and scale statistics for one or more multi-item scales. This program was written by David A. Specht while in the Department of Sociology at Iowa State University. For item analysis of Likert and semantic differential attitude scales the most relevant statistics from this program are alpha reliability coefficient, item correlations with total scale score, and item means and standard deviations. Other available statistics include matrices of interitem correlation and covariance and split-half reliability coefficient. The RELIABILITY subprogram does *not* also serve a scoring function. Scale scores for each respondent can be obtained by the use of subprogram COMPUTE. It is also necessary to implement a separate subprogram, FREQUENCIES, in order to output the distributions of responses for each item. Since SPSSX is an integrated system, these subprograms can easily be combined in a single program.

Input data are typically the raw data response matrix (respondents by items), but correlation or covariance matrices may alternately be input. Limitations of the program are the following: up to 50 scales may be analyzed at one time, from any combinations of items in the original pool; no less than 3 and no more than 500 items per scale; up to 1,000 items for all scales combined; no practical limit on the number or scoring of response categories; no practical limit on the number of respondents.

SPSS GUTTMAN SCALE

Subprogram GUTTMAN SCALE is designed for use in the construction and evaluation of Guttman scales. The item response matrix (respondents by items) is the required input data. Output includes the following:

1. Coefficient of reproducibility: 1 minus the proportion of errors (using a simplified variant of the Goodenough technique for counting errors)
2. Minimum marginal reproducibility
3. Percentage of improvement achievement by Guttman scale
4. Coefficient of scalability
5. Item intercorrelations and correlations with scale score

SAS

Like SPSS, Statistical Analysis System (SAS) is an integrated system of computer programs for data analysis. The SAS system, begun in 1966, has been one of the fastest-growing data analysis systems in popularity. In part, this is because of its relatively universal applicability across disciplines. In addition to statistical analysis capabilities, the SAS system has facilities for the management and modification of large data files, information storage and retrieval, and report writing. SAS was developed at North Carolina State University. It has attracted an international network of users, incorporated as the SAS Users Group, International (SUGI). *SAS Users Guide, Volumes I and II* (1981) are the primary users' manuals. Both of the programs described below are found in the *SUGI Supplemental Library Users' Guide* (1983).

SAS PROC ITEM

This is an item analysis program, similar to SPSS program RELIABILITY, except for one important restriction. PROCedure ITEM can be applied only to items with dichotomous scoring (such as cognitive test items, which are typically scored 1 or 0). While some affective instruments have dichotomously scored items (yes-no, agree-disagree, true-false), most attitude scales do not.

SAS PROC GUTTMAN

PROCedure GUTTMAN is very similar to SPSS GUTTMAN SCALE. Input is the matrix of responses by items. Output includes the following:

1. Scalogram: the data matrix, rearranged by item difficulty and respondents' scale scores to effect the characteristic triangular pattern of item and respondent scores
2. Coefficient of reproducibility (COR); this program uses the modified Goodenough technique, with the Proctor technique as an option
3. Minimum marginal reproducibility (MMR)
4. Percent of improvement: COR minus MMR

5. Coefficient of scalability (COS): percentage of improvement divided by (1 minus MMR)
6. Matrix of item intercorrelations and item correlations with total scale score

EDSTAT

EDSTAT is a library of packaged programs for statistical data analysis that first appeared in Veldman (1967). These programs were developed at the Research and Development Center for Teacher Education in the College of Education at the University of Texas.

EDSTAT TESTAT

Subprogram TESTAT is a test-scoring and item analysis program for multi-item scales. Up to nine separate scales can be handled at one time, totaling up to 150 items. (No item may be included in more than one scale.) If more than two scales are specified, a total (combined) scale is automatically scored and analyzed— whether or not this makes conceptual sense. Up to nine item response categories are allowable, scored from 1 to N. Scoring may be reversed for specified items.

Output from the program includes (1) scale scores for each respondent, (2) alpha coefficient for each scale, (3) distribution of responses for each item, (4) item and scale means and standard deviations, and (5) point biserial correlations of each item with its own scale score and with the total score from the combined scales.

EDSTAT TSCALE

Subprogram TSCALE computes favorableness (positiveness) values for Thurstone scale items by the method of successive intervals. These values are based upon judges' categorization of items into ranked favorableness categories. Resultant scale values are considered to be interval-level data. The program can handle up to 200 items with up to 11 favorableness categories.

References

Ajzen, I., & Fishbein, M. (1980). *Understanding attitudes and predicting social behavior.* Englewood Cliffs, NJ: Prentice-Hall.

Allport, G. W. (1935). Attitudes. In C. Murchison (Ed.), *Handbook of social psychology* (pp. 798–884). Worcester, MA: Clark University Press.

Allport, F. H., & Hartman, D. A. (1925). Measurement and motivation of a typical opinion in a certain group. *American Political Science Review, 19,* 735–60.

Beatty, W. H. (Ed.) (1969). *Improving educational assessment of an inventory of measures of affective behavior.* Washington, DC: Association for Supervision and Curriculum Development, National Educational Association.

Bogardus, E. S. (1925). Measuring social distance. *Journal of Applied Sociology, 9,* 299–308.

Bogardus, E. S. (1928). *Immigration and race attitudes.* New York: Heath.

Bogardus, E. S. (1931). *Fundamentals of social psychology* (p. 52). New York: Century.

Bogardus, E. S. (1959). *Social distance.* Yellow Springs, OH: Antioch Press.

Bonjean, C. M., Hill, R. J., & McLemore, S. D. (1967). *Sociological measurement: An inventory of scales and indices.* San Francisco: Chandler.

Bumke, O. (1911). *Die Pupillenstörungen, bie Geistes, und Nervenkrankheiten.* Jena, E. Ger.: Fischer.

Campbell, D. T. (1950). The indirect assessment of social attitudes. *Psychological Bulletin, 47,* 15–38.

Chun, K. T., Cobb, S., & French, J. R. P., Jr. (1975). *Measures for psychological assessment: A guide to 3000 original sources and their applications.* Ann Arbor: Institute for Social Research, University of Michigan.

Comrey, A. L., Backer, T. E., & Glaser, E. M. (1973). *A sourcebook for mental health measures.* Los Angeles: Human Interaction Research Institute.

Cook, S. W., & Selltiz, C. (1964). A multiple-indicator approach to attitude measurement. *Psychological Bulletin, 62,* 36–55.

Cooper, J. B., & Pollock, D. (1959). The identification of prejudicial attitudes by the galvanic skin response. *Journal of Social Psychology, 50,* 241–45.

Cronbach, L. S. (1951). Coefficient alpha and the internal structure of tests. *Psychometrika, 16,* 297–334.

Doob, L. W. (1953). Effects of initial serial position and attitude upon recall under conditions of low motivation. *Journal of Abnormal and Social Psychology, 48,* 199–205.

Dubin, S. S. (1940). Verbal attitude scores predicted from responses in a projective technique. *Sociometry, 3,* 24–28.

Edwards, A. L. (1957). *Techniques of attitude scale construction*. New York: Appleton-Century-Crofts.

Epstein, I. (1981). *Measuring attitudes toward reading*. Princeton, NJ: ERIC T/M, Educational Testing Service.

Ferneau, E. W., Jr. (1973). *Drug abuse research instrument inventory*. Cambridge, MA: Social Systems Analysts.

Fishbein, M. (1963). An investigation of the relationships between beliefs about an object and the attitude toward that object. *Human Relationships, 16*, 233–40.

Fishbein, M. (1967a). A behavior theory approach to the relations between beliefs about an object and the attitude toward the object. In M. Fishbein (Ed.), *Readings in attitude theory and measurement* (pp. 389–400). New York: Wiley.

Fishbein, M. (1967b). A consideration of beliefs, and their role in attitude measurement. In M. Fishbein (Ed.), *Readings in attitude theory and measurement* (pp. 257–66). New York: Wiley.

Fishbein, M., & Ajzen, I. (1975). *Belief, attitude, intention and behavior: An introduction to theory and research*. Reading, MA: Addison-Wesley.

Flanders, N. A. (1970). *Analyzing teaching behavior*. Reading, MA: Addison Wesley.

Gordon, R. L. (1977). *Unidimensional scaling of social variables: Concepts and procedures*. New York: Free Press.

Gump, R. (1962). *Jade: Stone of heaven*. New York: Doubleday.

Guttman, L. (1944). A basis for scaling qualitative data. *American Sociological Review, 9*, 139–50.

Guttman, L. (1950). The basis for scalogram analysis. In S. A. Stouffer, L. Guttman, E. Suchman, P. E. Lazarsfeld, S. A. Star, & J. A. Gardner (Eds.), *Measurement and prediction* (pp. 60–90). Princeton, NJ: Princeton University Press.

Hammond, K. R. (1948). Measuring attitudes by error choice: An indirect method. *Journal of Abnormal Social Psychology, 43*, 38–48.

Hartley, E. L., & Schwartz, S. (1948). *A pictorial doll play approach for the study of children's intergroup attitudes*. Unpublished manuscript, Research Institute in American Jewish Education, American Jewish Committee.

Henerson, M. E., Morris, L. L., & Fitz-Gibbon, C. T. (1978). *How to measure attitudes*. Beverly Hills: Sage Publications.

Hess, E. H. (1965). Attitude and pupil size. *Scientific American, 212*, 46–54.

Horowitz, E. L., & Horowitz, R. E. (1938). Development of social attitudes in children. *Sociometry, 1*, 301–38.

Indik, B. P., & Berrien, F. K. (1968). *People, groups and organizations*. New York: Teachers College Press.

Indik, B. P., Hockmeyer, M., & Castore, C. (1968). *A compendium of measures of individuals, groups, and organizations relevant to the study of organizational behavior* (Tech. Rep. No. 16, Nonr-404). New Brunswick, NJ: Rutgers, The State University.

James, W., & Lange, K. G. (1922). *The emotions*. Baltimore: Williams & Williams.

Johnson, O. G. (1976). *Tests and measurement in child development: Handbook II*. San Francisco: Jossey-Bass.

Johnson, O. G., & Bommarito, J. W. (1971). *Tests and measurements in child development: A handbook*. San Francisco: Jossey-Bass.

Kegan, D. L. (1970). *Scales/RIQS: An inventory of research instruments*. Evanston, IL: Northwestern University, Technological Institute.

Klukhohn, C. (1965). Values and value-orientations in the theory of action. In T. Parsons & E. A. Shils (Eds.), *Toward a general theory of action* (pp. 388–433). New York: Harper & Row.

Kuder, G. F., & Richardson, M. W. (1937). The theory of the estimators of test reliability. *Psychometrika, 2,* 151–60.

Kuethe, J. L. (1964). Prejudice and aggression: a study of specific social schemata. *Perceptual and Motor Skills, 18,* 107–15.

Kuntz, A. (1929). *The autonomic nervous system.* Philadelphia: Lea & Febiger.

LaPiere, R. T. (1934). Attitudes vs. actions. *Social Forces, 13,* 230–37.

Likert, R. (1932). A technique for the measurement of attitudes. *Archives of Psychology, 140,* 44–53.

Linton, R. (1945). *The cultural background of personality.* New York: Appleton-Century-Crofts.

Menzel, H. (1953). A new coefficient for scalogram analysis. *Public Opinion Quarterly, 17,* 268–80.

Mueller, D. J. (1970). Physiological techniques of attitude measurement. In G. F. Summers (Ed.), *Attitude measurement* (pp. 535–52). Chicago: Rand McNally.

Mueller, D. J. (1985). *The use of relative-belief items in the construction of attitude scales.* Unpublished paper, Indiana University.

Murphy, G., & Likert, R. (1937). *Public opinion and the individual.* New York: Harper & Row.

Murray, H. A. (1943). *Thematic apperception test manual.* Cambridge, MA: Harvard University Press.

Newcomb, T. M., Turner, R. H., & Converse, P. C. (1965). *Social psychology: The study of human interaction.* New York: Holt, Rinehart and Winston.

Osgood, C. E., Suci, G. J., & Tannenbaum, P. H. (1957). *The measurement of meaning.* Urbana: University of Illinois Press.

Pushkin, I. (1967). *A study of ethnic choice in the play of young children in three London districts.* Unpublished doctoral dissertation, London University.

Remmers, H. H. (1934). Generalized attitude scales: Studies in social-psychological measurement. In H. H. Remmers (Ed.), *Studies in higher education XXVI* (pp. 7–17). Lafayette, IN: Purdue University, Division of Educational Reference.

Remmers, H. H. (1960). *Manual for the Purdue Master Attitude Scales.* Lafayette, IN: Purdue Research Foundation.

Robinson, J. P., Athanasiou, R., & Head, K. B. (1969). *Measures of occupational attitudes and occupational characteristics.* Ann Arbor: Institute for Social Research, University of Michigan.

Robinson, J. P., Rusk, J. G., & Head, K. B. (1969). *Measures of political attitudes.* Ann Arbor: Institute for Social Research, University of Michigan.

Robinson, J. P., & Shaver, P. R. (1973). *Measures of social psychological attitudes.* Ann Arbor: Institute for Social Research, University of Michigan.

Rokeach, M. (1973). *The nature of human values.* New York: Free Press.

Rokeach, M., & Kliejunas, P. (1972). Behavior as a function of attitude-toward-object and attitude-toward-situation. *Journal of Personality and Social Psychology, 22,* 194–201.

Rosen, P. (Ed.). (1973). *Attitudes toward school and school adjustment, grades 4–6.* Princeton, NJ: Educational Testing Service.

Rosenberg, M. J. (1956). Cognitive structure and attitudinal affect. *Journal of Abnormal and Social Psychology, 53,* 367–72.

Rotter, J. B., & Willerman, B. (1947). The incomplete sentences tests as a method of studying personality. *Journal of Consulting Psychology, 11,* 43–48.

Saffir, M. A. (1937). A comparative study of scales constructed by three psychophysical methods. *Psychometrika, 2*, 179–98.

SAS Institute. (1982). *SAS users guide: Basics*. Cary, NC: Author.

SAS Institute. (1982). *SAS users guide: Statistics*. Cary, NC: Author.

SAS Institute. (1983). *SUGI supplemental library users guide*. Cary, NC: Author.

Schachter, S., & Singer, J. (1962). Cognitive, social and physiological determinants of emotional state. *Psychological Review, 69*, 379–99.

Shaw, M. E., & Wright, J. W. (1967). *Scales for the measurement of attitudes*. New York: McGraw-Hill.

SPSS Inc. (1983). *SPSSX users guide*. New York: McGraw-Hill.

Summers, G. F. (Ed.). (1970). *Attitude measurement*. Chicago: Rand McNally.

Taylor, J. B., & Parker, H. A. (1964). Graphic ratings and attitude measurement: A comparison of research tactics. *Journal of Applied Psychology, 48* (1), 37–42.

Thistlethwaite, D. (1950). Attitude and structure as factors in the distortion of reasoning. *Journal of Abnormal and Social Psychology, 45*, 442–58.

Thurstone, L. L. (1927). Psychophysical analysis. *American Journal of Psychology, 38*, 268-389.

Thurstone, L. L. (1928). Attitudes can be measured. *American Journal of Sociology, 33*, 529–54.

Thurstone, L. L. (1931). The measurement of social attitudes. *Journal of Abnormal and Social Psychology, 26*, 249–69.

Thurstone, L. L. (1946). Comment. *American Journal of Sociology, 52*, 39–50.

Thurstone, L. L., & Chave, E. J. (1929). *The measurement of attitude*. Chicago: University of Chicago Press.

Tittle, C. R., & Hill, R. J. (1967). Attitude measurement and prediction of behavior: An evaluation of conditions and measurement techniques. *Sociometry, 30*, 199–213.

Travers, R. M. W. (1941). A study in judging the opinions of groups. *Archives of Psychology*, No. 266.

Veldman, D. J. (1967). *FORTRAN programming for the behavioral sciences*. New York: Holt, Rinehart & Winston.

Walker, D. K. (1973). *Socioemotional measures for preschool and kindergarten children*. San Francisco: Jossey-Bass.

Wallen, R. (1943). Individuals' estimates of group opinion. *Journal of Social Psychology, 17*, 269–74.

Wicker, A. W. (1971). Attitudes versus actions: The relationship of verbal and overt behavioral responses to attitude objects. *Journal of Personality and Social Psychology, 19*, 18–30.

Wicker, A. W., & Pomazal, R. J. (1971). The relationship between attitudes and behavior as a function of specificity of attitude object and presence of a significant person during assessment conditions. *Representative Research in Social Psychology, 2*, 26–31.

Woodmansee, J. J. (1970). The pupil response as a measure of social attitude. In G. F. Summers (Ed.), *Attitude measurement* (pp. 514–34). Chicago: Rand McNally.

Zeligs, R. (1937). Racial attitudes of children. *Sociology and Social Research, 21*, 361–71.

Index

About the Author

DANIEL J. MUELLER, Associate Professor of Educational Psychology at Indiana University at Bloomington, teaches graduate courses in educational and psychological measurement, statistics, and social psychology. He earned his Ph.D. at the University of Illinois, where he studied with Norman Gronlund, Gene Glass, Gene Summers, and Martin Fishbein.

Mueller's research focuses primarily on measurement methodology. His research manuscripts have been published in such professional journals as *Educational and Psychological Measurement*, the *Journal of Educational Measurement*, the *Journal of Social Psychology*, the *Journal of Psychology*, and *Teachers College Record*. He has, in addition, published several critical reviews of standardized tests in measurement journals and reference books and has contributed to *Attitude Measurement*, a book of readings edited by Gene F. Summers.